Depression, Where Is Your Sting?

Depression, Where Is Your Sting?

Robert D. McBain

RESOURCE *Publications* • Eugene, Oregon

DEPRESSION, WHERE IS YOUR STING?

Copyright © 2021 Robert D. McBain. All rights reserved. Except for brief quotations in critical publications or reviews, no part of this book may be reproduced in any manner without prior written permission from the publisher. Write: Permissions, Wipf and Stock Publishers, 199 W. 8th Ave., Suite 3, Eugene, OR 97401.

Resource Publications
An Imprint of Wipf and Stock Publishers
199 W. 8th Ave., Suite 3
Eugene, OR 97401

www.wipfandstock.com

PAPERBACK ISBN: 978-1-7252-7964-3
HARDCOVER ISBN: 978-1-7252-7963-6
EBOOK ISBN: 978-1-7252-7965-0

02/23/21

Unless otherwise indicated, all Bible references are taken from the New King James Version®. Copyright © 1982 by Thomas Nelson. Used by permission. All rights reserved.

This book is for my beautiful wife, Joyce, and our adorable children, Joshua, Hannah-Rose, and Adalyn. Joyce's love and prayers and our children's smiling faces have been constant encouragements. This is for them. God is faithful.

And I find it kind of funny, I find it kind of sad
The dreams in which I'm dying are the best I've ever had.

—Roland Orzabal, "Mad World." In *The Hurting*. Mercury Records. LP. 1982.

Contents

Acknowledgments | ix

    Introduction | 1
1. What is Depression? | 11
2. What Depression Feels Like | 21
3. The Bible and Depression | 35
4. Rescued but not Resuscitated | 54
5. What is Health? | 65
6. Depression Returns | 78
7. The Church's Silence | 87
8. The Church's Response | 98
9. Depression: Round Two | 108
10. Fighting Depression Using the Psalms | 119
11. Depression, Where is Your Sting? | 130

    Afterword | 140

Bibliography | 141

Acknowledgments

I WANT TO THANK God first of all. Not once did I ever think I would author a book, especially not a book about a period of my life that I would rather forget. I am amazed at his graciousness and the patience with which he directed me over the years to bring me to this point. I pray he uses this book for his glory.

My wife, Joyce, is a constant inspiration. It was a big step for us to choose to walk in God's plan for our lives, but we embraced that call together. We have experienced blessings and challenges, but in each case, God always showed himself faithful. There is no one I would want to journey through life with and experience God's presence other than Joyce.

Woodlake Church is a blessing to our family. We are proud to call it our home. It is no exaggeration to say that we would never have made it this far without our church community's love, support, and prayers. I cannot stress this enough. If it were not for Woodlake, I probably would not be writing these acknowledgments today. Joyce and I thank God every day that our family has such a wonderful place to call home.

I would also like to thank all those who reviewed my manuscript and gave me feedback, no matter how brief. Kris Mineau, Dr. Wonsuk Ma, Dr. Nathan French, and Dr. Sally Shelton all helped. I genuinely appreciate their input and their encouragement in the process. I also thank Ben McIntyre because our impromptu conversation between church services one Sunday was the final push I needed to choose depression as my doctoral research topic. God orchestrated our conversation to become one of the main catalysts that led to this book.

Finally, I am deeply grateful to my mother. It was a cold January morning when we waved goodbye at Aberdeen airport to come to the USA and begin my doctoral journey. Separating her from some of her grandchildren, Joyce and I left her with a vacuum that only God knows. Nevertheless, God is faithful.

Introduction

A LIFE TO LIVE

My wife Joyce took these photos of our son Joshua and me one Scottish summer's day in 2015. I took the day off work, and we traveled thirty miles from our home to Aberdeen Pleasure Beach. It has fairground attractions, rides, restaurants, and is a brilliant place for a day out. The foremost reason we visited was to show Joshua the beach for the first time. We built sandcastles, looked for shells, and paddled in the surf.

The second picture does not show how a slight surge of water rolled in a few seconds later. Surprised, Joshua stepped back, but he was not too steady on his feet because he was only eighteen months old. He tripped over and fell backward. The sea submerged his body and splashed over his face. We thought the ordeal would put him off the sea for a while, but after we changed his wet clothes, his fascination with the sea and being on the beach soon returned.

Depression, Where Is Your Sting?

For me, the second picture carries much meaning. The sea stretches out before Joshua like the years of his life. Just like the sea, his life will pass through a few storms. He will experience uncertainty, turmoil, and inevitable loss. Like the sea, his life will have times of calm, fruitfulness, and adventure. I see the excitement in his eyes as he looks over the horizon, anticipating everything life has for him. But, beyond all the meaning I see in these pictures and my memories of the wonderful time we had that day, there lies a larger story. It is this larger story that makes the time we had together at the beach even more meaningful. What these pictures do not show is that about thirteen years before we visited Aberdeen Pleasure Beach that day—long before I met my wife Joyce and before Joshua was born—I tried to commit suicide at that very spot.

One crisp December night in 2002, I stood on Aberdeen beach, looking out onto the sparkling North Sea with only the stars and the full moon for companionship. My self-destructive lifestyle, anxiety, apathy, self-harm, and suicidal thoughts, all drove me towards this nexus. The pain and turmoil would soon end as the darkness I carried inside me, that swallowed

Introduction

all of life's goodness, would finally return to the deep. The universe chose me to die on that beach that night. I just needed the strength to walk into the numbing sea.

I thought I alone carried this pain and darkness. I believed that I was responsible for carrying the universe's missing piece, and by my sacrifice, I would return that piece and allow creation to reach its zenith. But I was wrong. Despite the drama and romantic poise with which I saw my life and forecast my demise, the devastating reality was that I was not that special. As I later discovered, the abyss I carried within me had a name—depression—and it did not reserve its pain only for me, for countless others suffered its pain as well.

Statistics show that depression affects 14.8 million people aged eighteen and older in America each year. That accounts for 6.7 percent of the US population,[1] and it costs the US economy $210.5 billion per year.[2] One source estimates that 15 percent of the US population will experience depression at least once in their lifetime.[3] Depression is so common that some describe it as the "common cold" of mental health problems.[4] Rates of depression increase substantially between thirteen and eighteen years of age.[5] One study found that depression accounted for 44 percent of pediatric mental health hospital admissions in 2009, costing $1.33 billion.[6] In 2015, 30 percent of high school students nationwide reported feelings indicative of depression, such as sadness and hopelessness.[7] Depression also causes other issues. Fifty percent of those with depression will have an anxiety disorder.[8] Depressed people are four times more likely to have a heart attack than those without a history of heart disease. They are more prone to suffer from sleep issues, appetite changes, decreased energy, concentration, and decision-making difficulties, signs of what appear to be retardation, and recurrent thoughts of death and suicide. Depression causes two-thirds of suicides.[9] It nearly caused mine.

---

1. Depression and Bipolar Support Alliance, "Depression Statistics."
2. National Network of Depression Centers, "Get the Facts."
3. Morin, "Depression Statistics Everyone Should Know."
4. Swinton, *Spirituality and Mental Health Care*, 95.
5. Avenevoli et al., "Major Depression in the National Comorbidity Survey," 37.
6. Bardach et al., "Common and Costly Hospitalizations."
7. Child Trends Databank, "Adolescents Who Felt Sad or Hopeless."
8. Morin, "Depression Statistics Everyone Should Know."
9. Depression and Bipolar Support Alliance, "Depression Statistics."

THE CHURCH'S SILENCE

Sufferers describe depression using terms like "hopelessness," "darkness," and "despair." Dorothy Rowe describes it as being like in isolation or prison.[10] Considering such metaphors are the antithesis of Christianity, we expect that Christianity, through its core message of hope, light, freedom, and victory over darkness, would fight off depression without effort. However, this is not the case. Rather than providing the shining light of Christ and embracing sufferers as it shows them the road to wholeness, Christianity's response through Christ's Body appears to be one of silence and stigma. For instance, Amy Simpson is a Christian author and mental health advocate who criticizes the church's response to mental illness as isolating, cruel, and not reflecting God's love.[11] In *Madness: American Protestant Responses to Mental Illness*, Heather Vacek describes how a cocktail of stigma and fear promotes silence and avoidance in the church.[12] Likewise, Ed Stetzer challenges the church to move past the whispering, the silence, the shame, and the stigma, and to join in Christ's mission by displaying His love.[13]

LifeWay Research's extensive survey exploring mental illness within America supports the assertions of these authors. The survey observed that although one in four Americans has a mental illness, many well-intentioned pastors and church leaders fail to inform their congregations about the issue.[14] According to one analysis of the survey, although 59 percent of senior pastors know someone with a mental illness diagnosis, only 66 percent of these pastors say they discuss the topic with their congregations.[15] To put it simply, this means that if we have 100 pastors standing in a row, 39 of them say they address the topic with their church. Even then, LifeWay's survey reveals a significant gap between what church leaders said their churches offered and what sufferers actually received.[16] Overall, the LifeWay survey noted:

- Few churches have plans to aid families affected by mental illness.
- Few churches have a counselor on staff skilled in mental illness.

---

10. Rowe, *Depression*, 1–3.
11. Simpson, "Mental Illness: What Is the Church's Role?"
12. Vacek, *Madness*, 3.
13. Stetzer, "The Church and Mental Health."
14. LifeWay Research, "Study of Acute Mental Illness and Christian Faith."
15. Smietana, "Mental Illness Remains Taboo Topic for Many Pastors."
16. Stetzer, "The Church and Mental Health."

- Most church leaders do not have training on how to recognize mental illness.
- Local churches are failing to tell their congregations what local mental health resources are available to them.
- There is a culture of silence, stigma, and shame within the church towards mental health.[17]

Although the silence of depression is a real problem within the church, with stigmatization arguably being the prominent response, the fact is that the church did not always respond in this way. In the past, the church was at the center of healthcare and healing, including depression and mental health. Centuries ago, those suffering from depression understood their illness and looked for healing through the church in a way that was consistent with their Christian worldview. But a cultural shift took place from the seventeenth century onwards that took mental illness out of the church's domain and placed it within the realm of biology and medicine.

As western culture developed, it came to understand depression as a "pathological psychological" condition, and it was routinely medicalized.[18] The effectiveness of pharmaceuticals in treating depression during the twentieth-century solidified this idea.[19] So, instead of looking to Christianity and the church to interpret and help them with their depression experiences, sufferers understood and explained their experiences using science and biology, and they looked to medicine for help.[20] The development of western culture led the church to believe that mental health was not its field. Where the church once had been at the center of mental health issues, changes in worldview pushed it to the periphery and determined its response, hence the church's silence.

On the upside, the church has shown a growing awareness of depression over the last few years. A cursory google of "church" and "depression" shows that more people are speaking against the silence. Some voices appear to criticize the church, assuming its silence results from deliberate apathy, but other voices speak redemptively. These voices try to coach the church into noticing the issue within its walls and suggest ways local

---

17. LifeWay Research, "New Study of Acute Mental Illness and Christian Faith"; Stetzer, "The Church and Mental Health."
18. Coudert, "Melancholy, Madness, and Demonic Possession" 678.
19. Taylor and Fink, *Melancholia*, 7.
20. Blazer, *The Age of Melancholy*, 11.

congregations can help those suffering in their communities. Despite these attempts, nothing seems to stir the church more than tragedy among its members. One example is the pastors of Saddleback Church, Rick and Kay Warren, whose son suffered from mental health issues and committed suicide in 2013. Saddleback Church responded by creating a new ministry called Hope for Mental Health.[21] The ministry model operates within local congregations and provides a discipleship program that seeks to present the friendship of Jesus to those struggling with mental health issues. Another unfortunate event occurred in 2019 when Jarrid Wilson, a mega-church pastor from California, committed suicide.[22] The irony of this event was that Wilson was an advocate for mental health, so his suicide caused church communities across America to raise their heads. In North Carolina, an affluent 6,400-member mega-church appointed a "Wellness Director" after experiencing six suicides in five years.[23] It is unfortunate, but nothing awakens the church quite like having to close the stable door after the horse has bolted. Despite the heartbreak, God redemptively uses these tragedies and the many others that do not make the headlines to push the church in the right direction and show Christ's healing love to those in need. I want to think that this book is my effort to help.

HOW I CAME TO WRITE THIS BOOK

Before becoming a Christian, I suffered from depression long before knowing that there was such an illness. My doctor diagnosed and prescribed antidepressants after my suicide attempt at Aberdeen Pleasure Beach. Despite the doctor continually increasing my dosage, my condition continued to deteriorate, and my life spiraled out of control into a vortex of self-destruction. During that tumultuous time, a religious experience in 2005 changed my life. I do not want to go into too much detail and give away my story so early, but I will say that my experiences with depression, the church, and God's healing power left me feeling responsible to sow back into God's Kingdom. Hence, the reason I author this book.

I began my Doctor of Ministry degree at Oral Roberts University, Tulsa, Oklahoma, in January 2017. My first idea for a doctoral research project concerned missions, but it did not feel like the correct topic. I

---

21. Saddleback Church, "Hope for Mental Health."
22. Stone et al., "Pastor and Mental Health Advocate Jarrid Wilson Dies by Suicide."
23. Garfield, "A Church Invests in Mental Health."

Introduction

always looked back to my depression experiences and wondered if I could use them to help others, but I had sunk two years of effort into the mission topic and did not want to begin over again. Still, thoughts continued to plague me of changing my research topic to depression. For months, 2 Corinthians 1:3–6 came to mind.

> Blessed be the God and Father of our Lord Jesus Christ, the Father of mercies and God of all comfort, who comforts us in all our tribulation, that we may be able to comfort those who are in any trouble, with the comfort with which we ourselves are comforted by God. For as the sufferings of Christ abound in us, so our consolation also abounds through Christ. Now if we are afflicted, it is for your consolation and salvation, which is effective for enduring the same sufferings which we also suffer. Or if we are comforted, it is for your consolation and salvation.

This passage spoke to me on many levels. I saw how the apostle Paul's experiences, whether good or bad, were for the church's wellbeing. When I connected my experience with depression into this passage, a sense of obligation filled my heart, compelling me to share my experiences to help those suffering.

Around the time I had to confirm my research topic with the doctoral committee, I bumped into a church friend who has experienced his own trials with ill health. We chatted, and he explained how he believes God used his experiences of suffering to help others have hope. This conversation struck a chord with me, and I knew what I had to do. I cast aside my doubts and began researching depression for my doctoral project. When it came time to publish my research project, I wanted to spice it up by including my depression experiences. I thought this would bridge the gap between the research and the reader and make it more palatable. I also wrestled with questions like, "Who is this book for?" and "Who do you want to read it?" My original goal was to write it for church pastors and leaders to inform them about depression and provide some suggestions to help them in their churches. But the more I struggled with those questions, the more I focused on the average Christian.

I visualized the average Joe or Jane taking part in the church service, distracted by their difficulties, and their efforts to worship hitting a wall of apathy. Their pastor's energetic preaching cannot penetrate the anguish that floods their minds. They may look rejuvenated in the church foyer after the service, but pain silently floods their hearts because they secretly suffer from depression. Either that or they maintain a brave face while they are in anguish about a child or other family member who suffers.

So, I wrote this book for them, for those who struggle through life between Sundays, not knowing if they have the strength to last another week. With this objective in mind, I included nothing from my doctoral research that did not help meet these goals. This meant that the story of my experiences and battles with depression came to define the book's content and took priority over my research.

THE BOOK'S OUTLINE

This book unites my story of depression with my doctoral research. It explores the history of depression and shows how the church was once at the heart of mental health issues, but the emergence of the biomedical model and the professionalization of healthcare moved the church to the periphery. Over time, western culture conditioned the church to be silent about the topic. However, the church has much to offer those struggling with depression. I examine some of those responses in this book, specifically how the church can respond to those in pain through hospitality and by imitating Jesus' style of friendship. Interventions, which in themselves, fit into the larger conversation of the Spirit's sanctifying role within the community and how he leads us to wholeness. This book also shows how the Psalms helped me in my battle with depression, which at an individual level, also corresponds to the Spirit's sanctifying work in my life as he led me to wholeness.

Chapter 1 describes my life growing up in a tiny fishing village on the east coast of Scotland and uses an industrial fishing accident to provide a metaphor for depression. It seeks to show the versatility and chameleonic nature of depression by showing how it is a multifaceted phenomenon. Depression is a disease (i.e., it is the absence of health), an illness (i.e., it has consequences known only to the sufferer), and a sickness (i.e., there are social consequences). When we see depression through these lenses, we can appreciate how comprehensive and convoluted it is.

Chapter 2 explores what it feels like to suffer from depression by interacting with John Swinton's study on the lived experiences of depression sufferers. Through extensive interviews and feedback sessions with depressed Christians, he identified key themes that ran through the subjects'

Introduction

experiences of depression. We interact with these themes by using my experience and research to paint a picture of what it is like to experience depression.

Chapter 3 tells the story of my self-harming. It acts as a bridge into the Bible by linking it with the demon-possessed man who sat among the tombs cutting himself. We discuss how depression and mental health are not silent issues within the Bible—a point substantiated by presenting a biblical approach to understanding depression. This chapter also offers a useful method for identifying depression in the Bible. These points help us see that since the Bible is not silent about depression, the church should not be silent either.

Chapter 4 tells the story of my suicide attempt and how my doctor diagnosed me by using the biomedical model to which society enculturated him. The biomedical model and its inability to view humans as beings that operate within the nexus of relationships is a stumbling block to developing a holistic approach to healing that can help people live fuller lives in the face of suffering. I argue that the biopsychosocial-spiritual model can help in this area because it recognizes humanity's spiritual dynamic and focuses on holism. The biopsychosocial-spiritual model acts as the foundation for this book because the biomedical model's empiricist foundation does not allow this underpinning.

Chapter 5 discusses western culture's view of health and the biblical view of health and argues that the west views ill-health as a deviation from personal and societal norms. Through a survey of society and culture, this chapter explains that the western view of health, compared to the Bible's perspective, is somewhat one-dimensional. The Bible sees health through the framework of *shalom* as something that encompasses all aspects of human life. The biomedical model's failure to see health in this regard meant that it did not have the resources to cure my depression—it took Jesus to do that. This chapter ends by telling my salvation testimony and healing from depression.

Chapters 6 and 7 tell the story of my first few years in the local church. I describe how the depression returned over the space of a few years. I speak about my local church experiences and note that the church was silent on mental health and depression. From this point, I present a brief historical survey describing why the church is silent. The survey shows how cultural changes and advancements in medicine and pharmaceuticals took mental illness and depression out of the church's domain and placed it within the medical field. Therefore, I argue that local churches typically are silent on depression because culture and society have taught them to be.

I develop chapter 8 upon the understanding that recent cultural changes have moved the church so that it is now in an excellent position to break the silence and help people suffering from depression. One way the church can help is by offering hospitality through Jesus-style friendships. This approach links into the Spirit's sanctifying role within the community and how he works through us as a missional community, thereby showing God's love to others through acts of mercy.

In chapter 9, I speak about my second bout of depression and describe what I did to overcome it. If the reader is looking for a place to skip to, this is probably the place. Chapter ten follows with a discussion of the Psalms of Lament. It describes how what I did in the ninth chapter to cure my depression was an age-old biblical technique, academically verified, for dealing with pain and suffering.

Chapter 11 draws the book to a conclusion by discussing how asking God for help and obediently acting upon the support he provides contributes towards our sanctification. I argue that I learned obedience and grew in Christlikeness through the life experiences that contributed to my depression and the healing I received by reading the Psalms. Furthermore, since the Spirit uses my suffering to help others, my story acts as a paradigm for how sanctification operates in the believer and the Christian community.

MY ROLE AS THE AUTHOR

I must be clear about my role as the author. Depression came upon me bit-by-bit during my mid-to-late teens, but I was about twenty-three or twenty-four when the doctor diagnosed me and prescribed antidepressants. Until receiving the diagnosis, I did not know depression existed as a health condition. I knew it was a word used to describe deep feelings of sadness or gloominess, but I never thought depression was something that someone may "have." For those five or six years before my diagnosis, I experienced the full effects of depression, but I never knew it even existed. I assumed my negative feelings and thoughts were part of my physical make-up. It was part of who I was, the way creation intended me to be, and there was nothing to blame. Therefore, I write in hindsight as I reflect on and interact with my depression experiences throughout the book. I play a double role as both a participant and an observer.

Introduction

This book is far from perfect. After every revision, there was so much I wanted to change and elaborate upon, but I had to stop somewhere, or I would never have finished. Through this process, though, I realized I feel this way about this book because it is very much a work in progress, and it probably will be for as long as I continue to reflect on my experiences. Nevertheless, even in its current state, it is my hope and prayer, as a Christian who suffered from depression, that this book helps others journey along their road to wholeness.

1

What is Depression?

RESCUED BUT NOT RESUSCITATED

I NEVER KNEW ROBERT Taylor, but I often thought of him as I conducted my doctoral research on depression in the USA. We both grew up in a tiny fishing village of about 1000 people called Pittenweem, situated within the East Neuk of Fife, which is on the East Coast of Scotland. Two words describe Pittenweem: fishing and tourism. The tourist industry is a later phenomenon brought on by the region's charm and by St Andrews, the Home of Golf, located nearby. Pittenweem features in the stories of the witch hunts that swept seventeenth- and eighteenth-century Britain. Google Books has a copy of *A True and Full Relation of the Witches at Pittenweem* in its database that was first published in 1704. It gives the account of and the investigation into five local women accused of witchcraft. Growing up there, it was common knowledge among us children that the burning of witches caused the scorch marks on the parish cemetery wall. Less macabre, but even more fantastic, were the tales of St. Filian, an ancient monk who lived in a cave near the parish church. His left hand used to glow as he sat in the darkness, so he could see to write his sermons. Indeed, Pittenweem, along with the entire region of the East Neuk of Fife, has a vibrant history. Even the father of the US Navy, John Paul Jones, bombarded the neighboring town in 1779.

I grew up with ghost stories, superstition, and tales from the deep—such things as one would expect from a small ancient village. However, despite the superstition and the folklore, commercial fishing is the trade that has sustained Pittenweem and the nearby seaside villages since humans first settled the area hundreds of years ago. Although now in decline, the fishing industry is the heart and soul of Pittenweem. For generations, my family was part of this village community. My father and grandfather both were fishing vessel owners and captains. So, it was only natural that I began working for my father as a commercial fisherman when I left school at sixteen. I did not know it then, but I entered the same work environment that had killed Robert Taylor decades earlier.

Long before I was born, Robert worked onboard one of my father's boats as a deckhand. Deckhands do the manual labor on board fishing vessels. They prepare the net, deck areas, and fishing equipment, and they gut and stow the catch. Their duties are exceedingly manual, taking place in some of the most grueling weather and unruly seas imaginable. Their work is a cold, wet, and lackluster affair, held together by camaraderie, their pay packet, and typically alcohol. In a working environment as tempestuous as the sea, dangers lie around every corner, and safety is always an issue. Hazards remain, no matter how many controls one puts in place to eliminate and reduce the risks. Robert was no exception. The tattered newspaper article I read many years later described how Robert fell overboard into the icy water. He was moving fish boxes on the open deck "when an unexpected movement of the boat threw him into the water. . . he was so numbed with the cold that he could not grab a lifebelt thrown within inches of him. . . the crewman pulled him on board within two minutes, but it was too late. Attempts to revive him by artificial resuscitation failed."

I imagined Robert's last moments. The wave blindsides the boat, toppling a heavy wall of water onto the deck, and the vessel keels over under the surge. Robert drops the fish box and staggers towards the rail. His hands flail, trying to grab something for support, but they catch empty air. He then experiences a brief feeling of extraordinary calm as his mind tries to catch up with the weightlessness he experiences.

Robert feels nothing but icy cold on the outside and the inside of his body—cold so sharp that it feels like a thousand knives stabbing every piece of warmth and air out of his body. Instinct does not let him breathe, nor does the icy darkness that surrounds him.

Heart and head pounding, Robert's arms scramble and claw to get back to the light, to the surface, and to the air. He bursts through and draws a harsh gasp, but his water-logged clothes pull him back under the water. Darkness surrounds him. Looking through bulging eyes, the surface shimmers just out of reach above him. His lungs and heart hurt with the yearning to inhale the fresh air, but the seawater is poison to him.

Again, he pushes through the surface. He coughs and chokes, his mouth overflowing with the taste of salt. He hears the noises of a motor rumbling and men shouting close by.

Robert is near his comrades. Yet the wave's ejection of him into the icy water, and into a struggle he would never have placed himself, isolates him from his crewmates. The numbing reality of the bitter environment separates him. It is hard to stay afloat, hard to breathe, and impossible to call for help. Those few moments of separation exhaust him. He goes back under. His vision is turning black from the outside-in. His lungs are on fire as he struggles to surface.

The crew gawks with despair over the boat's rail, watching Robert scrambling against the elements. They scurry here and there, grasping for a rope or a lifebelt. They see Robert's gulping mouth and white bulging eyes. "Grab this!" someone screams. Providence guides the lifebelt, and it lands within Robert's reach.

Robert's clumsy fingers fumble with the lifebelt's smooth surface. He is so overwhelmed by everything going on around him. It might as well have fallen yards away. He is cold, exhausted, and unable to receive the aid of those closest to him.

His crewmates rescue him, but they cannot resuscitate him. Robert was twenty-two years old when he died. The crisis into which life threw Robert killed him, but metaphorically, depression killed him.

I can associate with Robert. We were members of the same community, knew the same people, and worked in the same dangerous industry. I even worked with his brother for six years. But, the foremost reason I associate with Robert is that during my doctoral research on depression, many years later, I came to see Robert's accident as a metaphor for depression. I often wondered if amid the complex emotions surging through Robert's body—the horror, the separation, and the isolation—did any form of logical thought emerge? Did his rational mind ever catch up with the experiences rushing through his body to ask simple questions: "How did I get here? How do I get out? What is happening to me?" If Robert's mind processed such questions, it must have done so through a blur of shock and horror. This surge of emotion must have submerged any form of rational reflection in the same way that the icy water submerged his body. What

Robert experienced during his last moments could fit the scenario of many depression sufferers.

WHAT IS DEPRESSION?

Depression is a total body experience that isolates the sufferer from everything real.[1] It is a disorder that affects one's mind, behavior, body, and relationships. One source says it has caused more human suffering than any other disease.[2] The underlying causes of depression are complex. Episodes can range from mild to severe with some people only having one episode, while others may have many.[3] Yet, the feeling of imprisonment is one commonality running through them. Rowe says,

> Intellectually you know that you are sharing space with other people, that you are talking to them, and they are hearing you. But their words come to you as if across a bottomless chasm, and even if you can reach out and touch that other person, or that other person touches you, nothing is transmitted to you in that touch. No human contact crosses the barrier.[4]

Rowe uses imagery that shows the complexity of depression, revealing the separation between what sufferers know is happening and what their sense-experience tells them is happening. John Swinton says that this conflict forces them into a position where they feel abandoned and experience deep identity and existential issues.[5] He, therefore, describes depression as a profoundly spiritual experience, corresponding to a cataclysmic spiritual crisis that encompasses every part of the sufferer's life.[6]

That depression encompasses every part of the sufferer's life grounds our understanding of depression and makes us careful not to think of it as something immaterial that hovers around someone similar to a whim or wisp. Nor should we see depression as a kind of ethereal stimulus associated with melancholic eighteenth-century Romantic poets, brooding over their

---

1. Hart and Weber, *Unveiling Depression in Women*, 19.
2. Beck and Alford, *Depression: Causes and Treatment*, 4, citing Nathan S. Kline, "Practical Management of Depression," *Journal of the American Medical Association* 190 (1964) 732–40.
3. Hart and Weber, *Unveiling Depression in Women*, 19, 32–34.
4. Rowe, *Depression*, 1–2.
5. Swinton, *Spirituality and Mental Health Care*, 114–16.
6. Swinton, *Spirituality and Mental Health Care*, 131.

writing desks in the candlelit darkness. Rowe's description paints a vivid, earthy, and physical picture of depression. She uses verbs such as "talking" and "hearing." She refers to features natural to human expressions, such as "reach[ing] out" and "touch." If a child is sick, her mother strokes her forehead and sings to her to comfort her. When we see an old friend, we shake their hand or hug them. These, and the many other physical expressions, are what make us human. So, when we describe depression, we need to think of it as something that hinders the very earthy and physical features of what it means to be human. For instance, a depressed man receiving the warm hug of a friend might not feel the warmth of that friend's affection. A depressed young woman receiving a high-five and pats on the back from her teammates after scoring another fine goal might not experience the genuineness of their celebrations. Overall, depression is a fleshly and physical reality that creates a barrier that separates what the sufferer's intellect knows is happening from the things they actually experience.

Depression as a Disease

The medical model understands that depression is a disease, and consequently sees the experiences of sufferers as manifestations and symptoms of the disease.[7] The medical model approaches people as detached objects composed of systems, organs, cells, and biochemical reactions, that are open to scientific investigation.[8] Every facet of a person is measurable, body temperature being one example. Medical science states that normal body temperature ranges from 97°F (36.1°C) to 99°F (37.2°C). To the medical model, any deviation above or below this range might reveal an abnormality or a sign of dysfunction (i.e., a disease). Body Mass Index (BMI) is another example. It calculates a person's height and weight and tells them where they range on a scale from underweight to obese. By determining these measurable ranges, the medical model and healthcare professionals can assess whether people are healthy or unhealthy. Therefore, according to the medical model, a disease is a deviation from a determined biological norm.[9]

Psychiatry is a field of study and practice within the medical model whose specialty is diagnosing, preventing, and treating mental disorders.

---

7. Swinton, *Spirituality and Mental Health Care*, 146–47.
8. Sulmasy, "A Biopsychosocial-Spiritual Model," 24–25.
9. Helman, "Disease Versus Illness in General Practice," 548.

Psychiatry accepts that the patient and their environment are full of social, psychological, age, gender, and genetic stressors that may make someone vulnerable to depression. But, psychiatry does not accept that these factors cause depression. Psychiatry and the medical profession believe that depression is an innate biological abnormality or dysfunction that takes place in reaction to inherent factors (genetics, age, and gender) and environmental stressors (stress, grief, or relationships).[10] Depression, then, is the body's biological response to the stressors of life. So, according to the medical model, the root of depression is always biological.

In diagnosing depression as a disease (i.e., a deviation from a biological norm), psychiatrists and other healthcare professionals follow set diagnostic criteria that help them diagnose depression according to the patient's symptoms.[11] According to the American Psychiatric Association, common symptoms include the presence of a sad, empty, or irritable mood, accompanied by somatic cognitive changes that significantly affect the individual's capacity to act, which vary by duration, timing, or presumed cause.[12] These symptoms, which add up to the experiences of depression we spoke of before, are pathological manifestations of the disease, which psychiatry dismisses as symptoms of the biological problem. Other than acting as somatic symptoms that aid in diagnosis, their presence carries no inherent value. In fact, the absence of symptoms is desirable because their absence reveals the body is back to normal functioning.

Depression as an Illness

It might not be apparent, but a distinction exists between disease and illness. Cecil Helman describes disease as something an organ has and illness as something a person has.[13] The concept of illness goes beyond the medical understanding of disease as a physical abnormality or dysfunction and places the consequences of having the disease onto the sufferer and their personal environment. As Kenneth Boyd says, "[Illness] is a feeling, an experience of unhealth [sic] which is entirely personal, interior to the person of the patient." [14]

---

10. Blazer, *The Age of Melancholy*, 4, 8.
11. Blazer, *The Age of Melancholy*, 4–5.
12. American Psychiatric Association, *DSM-5*, 155.
13. Helman, "Disease Versus Illness in General Practice," 548.
14. Boyd, "Disease, Illness, Sickness, Health, Healing and Wholeness," 10.

Illness is the way a patient understands, experiences, and responds to their diagnosis of disease. Being ill or having an illness solidifies the experience of the disease at a practical, everyday level. Imagine a lady living with back pain for several years who lives and works around the discomfort. Finally, she goes to her doctor, who diagnoses her with osteoarthritis. She finds out that she will need constant medication, physiotherapy, and maybe surgery further down the line. The diagnosis forces her to reflect on her everyday activities and thereby affects her lifestyle. Besides the lifestyle reshuffle of having to take medication daily, she may hear from a friend about the benefits of yoga and pay for a membership at a nearby studio. She might venture into organic and whole foods and look at natural remedies. With these lifestyle changes, the illness may motivate her to adopt a healthier lifestyle. However, even if the illness brings some benefits, most lifestyle changes will be negative and limit her everyday activity. Before, she grinned through the pain and did her best. Now, she avoids certain activities and movements altogether. Going on the bone-jarring rollercoaster with her grandchildren is no longer an option. For her, the disease of osteoarthritis has affected her lifestyle and the way she interacts with her environment. The disease has become an illness.

Illness is a personal phenomenon dependent upon our individual perspectives of ill-health.[15] We construct the way we experience illness around our own perspectives, personalities, and cultural and social backgrounds. Social influences at work in our culture shape our understanding of a disease by conditioning us how to experience, perceive, and cope with it. Because of this, our cultural beliefs influence how we behave when we are ill, thereby affecting how we describe our symptoms, whom we go to for care, and how we evaluate that care. These factors influence the emotional meaning we place on the illness and how we respond to the diagnosis and symptoms. Our personalities and our social and cultural backgrounds even affect how we react to pain.[16] So, with our example, the lady is not experiencing and responding to her osteoarthritis in a vacuum. Instead, she experiences and reacts to her illness relative to how culture and society have conditioned her to react.[17] The same holds for depression sufferers.

---

15. Helman, "Disease Versus Illness in General Practice," 548.
16. Helman, "Disease Versus Illness in General Practice," 549.
17. Kleinman et al., "Culture, Illness, and Care," 141.

In a study among South Asian women living in the UK, researchers observed that sufferers culturally interpreted their depression experiences.[18] This finding coincides with research among Pentecostals, which noticed that sufferers described depression subjectively.[19] Therefore, it is evident that there is a certain amount of relativism involved in the experience of depression. This explains why it is not unusual for sufferers to self-diagnose. Indeed, this is what my doctoral research suggested. On average, 50 percent of people who answered my survey and said they had depression, had not received a medical professional's diagnosis.[20] I expected this result based on the understanding that depression is culturally constructed and subjective. In a way, sufferers do not require a healthcare professional's diagnosis because the contextual and relativive nature of the illness allows sufferers to self-diagnose.

Depression as a Sickness

Since illness is a social and cultural construct that affects the patient's understanding and experience of a disease at a personal level, then the term "sickness" corresponds to the way society sees the illness. Although the patient is part of society, sickness is a designation society places on the patient that is external to the patient's own understanding of the illness. Because society defines sickness, society also determines a sick person's position within the community. Within this fluid context, the patient experiences sickness as a role they must negotiate within society.[21] Since our western culture sees health as a social ideal by believing we need it to function normally in life,[22] the lady with osteoarthritis may begin to view herself negatively—especially if her condition deteriorates to the extent that she can no longer function as she used to among her friends and social settings, or with her colleagues at work. She may come to believe that she has very little value since she can no longer function within her social circle in the way that society at large says she should. Should things worsen, and she has to give up work and claim social security because of losing her job and health insurance, society may

---

18. Fenton and Sadiq-Sangster, "Culture, Relativism and the Expression of Mental Distress," 81–82.
19. Trice and Bjorck, "Pentecostal Perspectives," 283.
20. McBain, "Exploring the Silent Nature of Depression," 131–32.
21. Boyd, "Disease, Illness, Sickness, Health, Healing and Wholeness," 9–17.
22. Swinton, "Understanding Health."

view her as a burden. In seeing her and others in similar situations, society is defining her condition and placing on her a label that is external to her own understanding and experience of the disease.

Some societies will be more tolerable of some sicknesses than others, and the labels that come with sicknesses may either be burdensome or liberating for the sufferer.[23] For example, someone with cancer may say, "I'm battling cancer." A charity may publicize, "Join us on the war against cancer." Battle imagery infuses these terms. They refer to cancer as something to fight. In doing this, people with cancer dissociate themselves from the disease. It is something they must defeat and repel. In a way, society's use of such militant language reveals society sees no shame in having cancer. Even if sufferers lose the battle, their family and friends still speak of them as heroes, having fought bravely: "They never gave up."

On the other hand, diseases such as AIDS and sexually transmitted diseases (STDs) carry with them an element of shame. Society does not hold sufferers of these diseases in such high esteem as those who have cancer. Notice boards in doctors' waiting rooms assure sufferers of their anonymity. The societal shame these diseases carry makes it difficult for sufferers to talk openly. This means that the sufferer has to bear the shame and the societal baggage along with the disease. We will seldom hear anyone boast of battling their STD at a church testimony night.

Depending upon the mental health condition, the level of societal labeling will differ. Depression tends to hide under the radar and remains unseen in many cases. However, because medicine considers depression an illness of the mind and categorizes it alongside other mental illnesses, society tends to brand it negatively as a condition that brings shame and embarrassment. This is inevitable because, as Jan Dewing says, our western society holds a high opinion on the mind.[24] Writing on the topic of personhood and dementia, she provides her readers with a historical summary to show how western thought over the last few hundred years has elevated the mind above every other facet of being human. This means that if a person loses their mind, they lose the fundamental part of their personhood that makes them uniquely human. In a society like ours, which values the mind above other factors, when someone loses their mind or a part of it, they literally lose a part of their humanity. Therefore, it is not surprising that being mentally ill is something that people do not typically want to admit.

---

23. Boyd, "Disease, Illness, Sickness, Health, Healing and Wholeness," 9–17.
24. Dewing, "Personhood and Dementia," 5.

Summary

Depression is a multifaceted phenomenon. It is a disease (i.e., biological dysfunction causing health's absence), an illness (i.e., it has consequences known only to the sufferer), and a sickness (i.e., it carries a social label). We can appreciate that depression is a comprehensive and sophisticated phenomenon when we see it through these lenses. But we must be careful not to regard diseases and illnesses as distinct entities in themselves. Instead, they are models that allow us to understand the different dynamics at play as we seek to understand depression or any illness. Because of this, I sometimes found it difficult to stick to a strict terminology throughout this book, so sometimes I refer to these three terms (disease, illness, and sickness) interchangeably.

2

What Depression Feels Like

"HERE THEY BE MONSTERS"

I REMEMBER LEAVING ABERDEEN harbor and going to sea for the first time when I was sixteen. I looked back over the vessel's stern to see the mouth of the harbor slowly close behind us—the red oil rig supply vessels at berth and the enormous white gas and oil cylinders on the quay steadily receded. I saw Aberdeen Pleasure Beach running north up the coast, with the fairground rides moving in the distance. People walked on the beach, couples held hands, others kicked a soccer ball about on the yellow sand, and some braved the cold water and paddled in the surf. I saw a couple building a sandcastle with a toddler. His busy little hands stopped to point at our boat. I waved, but I do not think he saw me.

 Everything was moving out of reach. It all seemed distant. I wanted to be among those people and enjoy whatever it was they were enjoying. The ice cream, the paddling, and building sandcastles—I wanted to be with them, but I was leaving to enter an unfamiliar world. I might not have been looking out over the star-filled horizon and taking my first step into a galaxy far-far-away, but in my little way, I was entering a realm that few experience—I was entering the exciting and dangerous world of the deep-sea fisherman. I imagined an ancient worn sea chart with indecipherable scribblings in black ink all over it, and expanses labeled "unexplored." A grizzly pirate hand points a crooked finger at an outline of a sea-serpent at the tattered corner of the chart. "Here they be monsters," he says in a deep gravelly voice.

What Depression Feels Like

I never stared with terror into the black beady eyes of the Great White Whale or saw the Kraken emerge from the deep to devour an entire ship. I never had to struggle against the lure of beautiful sirens as they called to forlorn sailors out of the nighttime fog, but during my six years as a fisherman, I found my own monster more malevolent than the rest. It crept up on me, wrapped its wispy tendrils around my soul, and infiltrated my life one calculated inch at a time, at a pace so slow that by the time I noticed, it had grown into an unquenchable void.

I was part of a loving and healthy family. As a commercial fisherman, I earned lots of money and had excellent career prospects. I had many friends and a robust social network. Everything was going well for me, and I had every reason to smile and enjoy life. But these favorable qualities did not stop the monster from vacuuming up life's goodness. Like a parasite, the more happiness it devoured, the larger it grew. It suffocated everything I had to live for and enjoy. It devoured every sliver of light and joy in my life and left behind a complex web of negative thought patterns and emotional systems in its wake. These dominated my life.

I became unhappy with life. After six years, spending ten or eleven days away from home, washing back and forth on the open sea commercial fishing no longer seemed a fruitful long-term venture. I could not envision myself doing this for another forty years like my dad. And what life, happiness, and joy I had, sunk into the same depths from which we caught our fish. As a fisherman, I took life from the sea for profit, but it took back a little of mine in exchange. Things grew unbearable and leaving the family business to do my own thing seemed the only escape. Hearing of the wonders of student life, I went to the University of Aberdeen. I figured that it was far enough away from home to do whatever I liked, yet close enough to come home now and then. Plus, I was familiar with Aberdeen because it had a large commercial fishing fleet, and our boat launched from there and landed our fish there.

I left high school with no qualifications, which meant that I had to complete an access program to get accepted. The university access program was a twelve-week full-time intensive program that took place during the summer term. I had to move from home and stay in the Hillhead Halls of Residence with other students. Many of them were high schoolers who, for various reasons, did not get the grades they needed for the university to accept them, so they took this access program to make up their grades or as an alternative route into the university. Others were older and, like me, wanted another chance at education, hoping to make something of their lives the second time around. In hindsight, putting a group of energized teenagers in with a bunch of people who mostly had a track record of procrastinating and making the wrong choices was not the best mixture for productivity. Well, it produced something, but probably not the grades the program coordinators expected. As far as I and those I befriended in the program were concerned, the program was a drunken revelry of endless partying and sleepless nights. For example, most weekdays we had a math lecture at 9 am (or "maths" as the British call it). To get there was a twenty-minute walk from our dorms through the greenery of Seaton Park. Often we went to the lecture having had no sleep because we spent the whole night drinking.

After scraping through the access course, the partying I experienced during the program did more than prepare me for university studies: it prepared me for student life—a life in which every night was a raucous party so long as there was money, and we ingeniously stretched what we had. I turned away nothing and took part in pretty much any opportunity to try something new. In some way, I felt that leaving high school at sixteen and entering the adult world of commercial fishing had robbed me of my teenage years. This was my opportunity to relive them.

I enjoyed this new refreshing life to the max. I had no goal or destination in mind. I only chose a degree in Computing Sciences and Mathematics because I enjoyed playing video games. But, with my intense drinking schedule, there was no way that I would ever read that 1000-page JavaScript book, and it would be a cold day in hell before I woke in time to go to a 7 am Advanced Calculus lecture. This behavior perhaps explains why I flunked every class in my first year, except an Organizational Management class. However, I did not see things like that. To me, I failed because my degree required too much study—I mean, who goes to university expecting to study? I changed degrees and switched over to History of Art, which fitted my lifestyle better and fulfilled my genuine interest in history.

I would not have described my lifestyle as self-destructive, although looking back now, it was. Nor did I ever consider that my behavior tilled the soil for a harvest I was not prepared to reap. With such a lifestyle, though, it was inevitable that the monster I brought back from the deep would reappear. I imagine it looked around for me back in Pittenweem, figured out where I was, and came to find me—and find me it did. I had created the perfect habitat amid the drink and the revelry for it to thrive and consume me.

THEMES OF DEPRESSION

I do not want to go into too much detail about my life with depression. Instead, I will let Swinton's research do the talking to provide a picture of what it is like to suffer from depression. Through interviews and feedback sessions with depressed Christians, Swinton identified themes running through their experiences, which describe the reality of depression for many sufferers. In this section, I present these themes and interlace them with my experience and research to paint a picture of depression. In doing this, I hope that those who have never experienced depression might gain a glimpse into its nature, while those who have suffered from it might find some comfort and support in the knowledge that others have experienced the same thing. In any case, I pray that by delving a little into depression's depths, we might gain insight into the magnitude of the redemptive work of Christ as he leads us towards wholeness.

Meaninglessness

Others have described what I experienced during this period of my life by using similar terms such as "abyss," "nothingness," "void," and "darkness." These terms convey a certain sense of meaninglessness which, according to Swinton, is a central theme of the depression experience.[1] Meaning is essential to our wellbeing and is foundational to positive mental health. Meaningfulness and purpose act as a framework through which we interpret and process life events, so when hardship and trauma strike, our life's meaning helps us cope. This is true even for those who suffer from depression. If sufferers can recognize their lives still have purpose, then they have more healthy patterns of dealing with the difficulties that depression causes. However, suppose their support structure of meaningfulness erodes or shatters. In that case, this loss leaves them facing many challenges. They lose their ability to handle adverse life events and foresee positive outcomes.[2]

---

1. Swinton, *Spirituality and Mental Health Care*, 113.
2. Swinton, *Spirituality and Mental Health Care*, 112–13.

I experienced profound meaninglessness when I suffered from depression. But, if I was to remember back before I began experiencing depression's symptoms, I cannot pinpoint a time when my life ever had meaning or purpose. I remember floating around as a child and teen, doing the things people of those age groups do. I played with my friends, went to school, watched TV, and the like, but I cannot remember ever considering my life's meaning and purpose. Maybe, back then, I was at a stage in my childhood and adolescent development where I was too immature to consider such things. Still, I often wonder if depression was maybe not to blame for the meaninglessness I felt in my life; perhaps depression magnified what was already absent. If depression brought meaninglessness to my life by revealing what was missing, then maybe it did so by forcing me onto another developmental stage within which it was natural for me to begin asking some of life's more existential questions.

Questions about the Meaning of Life

Questioning life's meaning was a characteristic that Swinton observed among his research participants. He noted that depression made them question everything they once found true, and by questioning, they lost faith in those things they previously believed. This led them to lose hope and meaning. One of Swinton's interviewees says,

> "I didn't actually consider it [life's meaning] properly until I got depression, because when my mood was low, my thought processes were wrong, that made me question really everything about myself and about my life and about the whole thing."[3]

In this person's case, we can see how depression can force sufferers to question their worldview. "Worldview" is a term used to describe how people see the world. It is an encompassing term that takes into consideration everything that matters to the person. It describes their fundamental beliefs about the world, the universe, and their role in it. As James Sire says, "[Worldview] Is a set of pre-suppositions (assumptions that may be true, partly true, or entirely false) which every person holds (consciously or subconsciously, consistently or inconsistently) about the basic make-up of the world."[4]

---

3. Swinton, *Spirituality and Mental Health Care*, 113.
4. Sire, *The Universe Next Door*, 17.

A person's worldview shapes and informs their experience of the world around them. It determines their opinions about events and helps them interpret their experiences within the larger social environment in which they exist. Worldview plays an essential role in defining a person's life. It shapes what they believe, how they act, and it gives their life meaning and purpose. Worldview does not just develop overnight. It forms through the generations and is conveyed through society, community, and family units. Because of the essential role that worldview plays in someone's life, when depression forces someone to question their worldview, it can have dramatic consequences related to their identity formation.

Depression's influence makes sufferers question their worldview. Yet, this questioning process does not seem to come from the sufferer's own volition. Notice in the above quotation that the interviewee said depression "made me question." So, in some way, sufferers do not consider themselves responsible for initiating the questioning process. This is the opposite of what we experience in academia. Academia encourages students to question and to probe their worldview to develop and enrich it, but this questioning is an act of volition. The student engages in this process voluntarily. For the depression sufferer, however, the questioning process seems motivated less by choice and more by duress.

The way depression forced me to question my reality and those things I held dear took place in a way that did not destroy my belief system, probably because I had none. Instead, I more so questioned the integrity of relationships, my self-worth, and the value of living. The questions depression caused me to ask did little to dissolve my worldview and did more to spark a search for truth. When I say, "search for truth," I am not referring to an intense search for truth like a John Grisham novel. My search for truth was more of a "search for something else."

For example, I randomly bought the *Spirit-Filled Life Study Bible* when I was seventeen. As it happened, I met some of the contributors years later when I went to the USA to study. Back then, though, when I bought it, I read it from cover to cover twice in one year. I do not know what I expected to happen as a result, but nothing happened at all. Another instance is from when I was in my early twenties, during my undergraduate studies. I read a book called *An Introduction to Buddhism* and began practicing meditation. I do not mean to offend anyone, but it was a joke. When you are plying yourself full of cheap vodka and staying awake until the small hours of the morning going to bars and clubs, transcendental meditation kind of loses its edge. Tarot and the Ouija board were other avenues I explored. I followed their instruction books with ignorant compliance and became proficient at providing private readings. I remember even sleeping with the tarot cards under my pillow, which was what the instructions said to do. But, I cannot say they, or anything else I tried, answered life's questions or pacified the darkness that permeated my life. The only things that helped me were self-harming and drinking. Drinking numbed the pain, and self-harming took the pain away for a few moments. I am not sure to what extent these contributed towards my "search for something else." Rather, they seemed to act as some form of retribution, in the sense that if the universe chose me to carry this burden, then the least I could do was engage whole-heartedly in the suffering it demanded from me.

Feelings of Abandonment

The questions depression asked of me and my search for meaning (if you want to call it that) made me feel abandoned. This abandonment was not a slight, transient feeling. It was a deep feeling that made me think creation had sovereignly chosen to abandon me. Remember, I did not know depression existed or that others were suffering from depression. My thinking was so warped. I thought I was the "chosen one" who had been called before the dawn of time to bear the negative thoughts, feelings, and experiences that depression laid upon me. I thought I was special. Ultimately, this idea that I was special resulted from the fact that looking outside myself for answers proved futile, so I began looking inside myself. When I looked inside myself for answers, the only thing I found was my ego. Upon finding my ego, I elevated myself up to a place where I became my reality and considered myself, if in a deflated and self-diminutive way, someone who was special. Within the context of my experiences of depression, I looked to myself for answers. But, I was not that special because countless other people had and were experiencing the same thing.

Swinton interviewed some of these people and observed how they experienced abandonment in two ways: abandonment by God and abandonment by others. Swinton carried out his study among Christians, and he noticed that feeling abandoned by God caused identity issues for the sufferer. He describes how a Christian's understanding of faith corresponds to living in a relationship with God. As with any relationship, it involves the intellect and emotions. What happens with depression is that it obstructs the emotions that emerge from the relationship. This means the sufferer can no longer experience God, or any relationship, in the way they are accustomed. The inability to experience relationships causes sufferers to feel abandoned and deep existential issues in Christians.[5] I would assume this is especially true for those from Christian traditions who have a continued expectation of the experience of God in helping them understand and interpret their everyday lives (we will talk more about this in later chapters). As Swinton says, "If a person can no longer relate to God, and if their self-image and interpretation of the world depends on their experience of God, then to experience such abandonment is, in a very real sense, to lose part of themselves."[6]

My first experience with depression took place before I became a Christian. Because I did not think God existed, I had no genuine feeling that God had abandoned me. Even if he did exist, I was sure he would not concern himself with someone like me. So, wondering whether God had abandoned me never crossed my mind, but I still felt alone and desolate. I considered myself like one who walked the street on a gloomy, rainy day. Everyone else took shelter in the warmth of cafes and bars, as well as under awnings or umbrellas, but not me. I had to walk alone in the wintry bleakness with the warm lights from the shop windows not casting their glow on me. That was how I experienced abandonment. God had not abandoned me, because he did not exist. Instead, I saw myself as one who had to wander alone through a life of darkness, bearing a weight that had no name or source.

The Feeling of "Clinging On"

Swinton's participants reported that although they felt adrift in a sea of meaninglessness, confusion, and desolation, they still held on to the hope of a better future. They still had a "reason to be." Swinton relates this theme to his participants' strong desire to keep alive some residue of their connection with God, even though depression sought to dissolve everything around them. Nevertheless, a person cannot hold on forever, and their strength will eventually wane.[7] For the non-Christian, as for the Christian, the motivating factor compelling them to hold on might be their friends

---

5. Swinton, *Spirituality and Mental Health Care*, 114–16.
6. Swinton, *Spirituality and Mental Health Care*, 115.
7. Swinton, *Spirituality and Mental Health Care*, 117.

or family, or another obligation. Naturally, a sufferer's ability to hold on is connected to their ability to interpret their depression experiences positively and to see the light at the end of the tunnel. However, if they lose sight of that hope, or should depression extinguish the light, then the sufferer's "reason to be" may reverse and leave behind a wish to "un-be."[8] This desire to "un-be" corresponds with suicidal thoughts and actions, as well as other activities that are not in the sufferer's best interest. Some examples are self-harming, extreme negative thought patterns, and other behavior patterns that go against the grain of what we would readily consider as positive behavior.

I am sure we have heard appeals—if not in actual life, then on film and TV—from sympathizers to their depressed loved ones to assess how their suicide will affect their friends and family. "Think things through," they say. "What about your loved ones? They'll miss you. How will they cope without you?" Or "Think of the bigger picture. You have so much to live for." These petitions, and the many others, try to appeal to the sufferer's sense of restraint and obligation to make them realize that there are people present who love and care for them.

Years ago, I looked at a chat forum about suicide on the internet. One person commenting was part of a forensic clean-up crew. He worked crime scenes, car accidents, and things like that. If there was a biological mop-up required, he was part of the team that cleaned it. Sometimes, he even cleaned up suicide scenes. On the forum, he went into detail about one job he was on in which a suicide victim blew his head off with a shotgun. The man on the forum spoke of scrubbing blood off the carpet, cleaning brain splatter off the ceiling and the walls, and using tweezers to pick embedded teeth and bone fragments out of the wall and ceiling plaster. He concluded by asking this question, "Imagine the effects this gruesome suicide scene had on the family member who walked in to discover the body?" He meant his description of the horrible scene and rhetorical question to deter those considering suicide. However, as well-intentioned as the man's graphic description was, for someone intent on suicide, I doubt that this man's appeal would deter them because, when someone truly decides to "un-be," it takes more than pleas to their sensibilities to stop them. This man's appeal would

---

8. Mark Altschule links this desire to "un-be" with deep despair. He parallels it with Judas Iscariot's betrayal of Jesus and suicide. See Altschule, "The Two Kinds of Depression According to St. Paul," 779–80.

only inform the person who had decided to commit suicide to choose the method wisely. At least that is what I would have done.

I often thought of my family and how they would cope and grieve, knowing I committed suicide. But, the pain depression caused in my soul was unbearable. I did not care about the predicament in which I would leave my family. I just wanted the pain to go away. However, I was fortunate, because once my doctor diagnosed me, the medication stopped me from acting upon my wish to un-be, albeit by creating a false psychological reality.

One reason appealing to the sufferer's sensibilities is not compelling is because depression sufferers often operate within paradoxes. Aaron Beck and Brad Alford notice that a disparity exists within many sufferers between their images of themselves and the objective facts. To explain what they mean, Beck and Alford use the examples of the wealthy woman moaning she does not have the finances to feed her children, or the prize-winning physicist who criticizes and calls himself stupid. These cases are two examples where the depressed person's behavior does not line up with the facts. Appeals and demonstrations to reason often do little to sway depression sufferers. Instead, sufferers behave unreasonably, performing acts that enhance their suffering. The wealthy man who puts on rags and humiliates himself in public by begging for money, or the faultless clergyman who tries to hang himself because he assumes he is the world's biggest sinner, are examples. These show how paradoxical the behavior and attitudes of sufferers can be. The reason such behavior is paradoxical, according to Beck and Alford, is because it goes against the "pleasure principle," which says humans should seek to maximize satisfaction and minimize pain. As they say, "According to the time-honored concept of the instinct of self-preservation, they [depression sufferers] should be attempting to prolong life rather than terminate it."[9]

I can relate to Beck and Alford's idea of depression being a paradox, because I operated within similar paradoxes. I had money, was handsome (at least my wife thinks so), had a career, and had loving family and friends. I had everything going for me in the grand scheme of things, yet I dressed in rags and had no self-worth. I embraced my suffering and owned it in a way contrary to the pleasure principle.

---

9. Beck and Alford, *Depression: Causes and Treatments*, 3.

Physical and Psychological Exhaustion

I mentioned above that a sufferer's ability to hold on to life remains only so long as they are strong enough not to let go. This battle causes physical and psychological exhaustion that weakens the sufferer's resolve and makes relationships very difficult. Swinton says depressed people isolate themselves, not because they do not want the company, but because they lack the strength, confidence, and motivation to make the effort to build relationships. He describes this phenomenon as a strange paradox in which depressed people want to relate to others, yet they experience the need to distance themselves from other people.[10] Describing her own experience of the effects of depression on her personal life, one lady said:

> "At first, I'd try to explain that it's not really negativity or sadness anymore, it's more just this detached, meaningless fog where you can't feel anything about anything—even the things you love, even fun things—and you're horribly bored and lonely, but since you've lost your ability to connect with any of the things that would normally make you feel less bored and lonely, you're stuck in the boring, lonely, meaningless void without anything to distract you from how boring, lonely, and meaningless it is."[11]

The way depression dissolves personal relationships is problematic because a person experiencing depression does not have the resources to sustain themselves in isolation. Sometimes the only way they can find the strength and the support they need to endure and to have hope is by their community sustaining them.[12] I understand the word "community" not only to mean the local church, parent-child, or marriage/partner relationships, but also social structures of every kind, including the workplace and anywhere else that requires social engagement. Depression's nature of isolation hobbles sufferers from finding the sustenance they need because it isolates them from themselves and community nourishment. As bad as this is, it may not be a terrible thing because the dysfunction and impairment that depression causes in the sufferer's social life, family, work, education, etc., can force sufferers to seek help.[13] For example, missed days and low productivity at work may destabilize the sufferer's job performance and

---

10. Swinton, *Spirituality and Mental Health Care*, 117–19.
11. Durbin, *Depression 101*, 106.
12. Swinton, *Spirituality and Mental Health Care*, 117–19.
13. Durbin, *Depression 101*, 115–16.

force them to seek treatment to fulfill their duties and keep their job. The destabilizing behavior their depression causes on family relationships may also compel depression sufferers to seek help.

Feeling Demoralized and Trapped into Living

The ongoing battle with depression leaves sufferers demoralized. They become physically and psychologically exhausted and lose the will to live. Swinton quotes an interview with one of his participants. Her testimony displays a deep tension in which she experiences periods of God's love and rejoices in his presence. Yet, she is furious and resents God because she feels he is preventing her from killing herself. This lady, and others like her, are trapped into living and believe God is preventing them from considering "the most logical and rational way of ending the psychological pain."[14] Swinton explains,

> The knowledge of being loved by God provides the strength to cling on in times of deep distress. However, at the same time, the fear of that same God acts to prevent self-harm, even though self-harm may be the desire of the individual and the best perceived solution. Life with depression is lived in the midst of this tension between being pleased about being alive, and a feeling of being 'stuck in life', an experience which can be both frustrating and at times annoying.[15]

The act of suicide for the depressed person is a reasonable response, but their relational structures and belief system often stop them from performing that action. Fear of God and what their religious tradition teaches about where suicide victims spend eternity usually dismiss suicide as a viable opt-out for many Christians. Therefore, suffers often feel trapped into living. As Swinton says, a depressed person has mixed feelings about being alive and being dead, which may cause severe psychological and physical suffering when united with the sufferer's theology of depression.

Beck and Alford observe that thoughts of suicide, or "suicidal wishes," are historically associated with depression. Seventy-four percent of severely depressed people report suicidal thoughts. These thoughts may manifest in a variety of ways, from being a "passive wish" ("I wish I were dead"), an

---

14. Swinton, *Spirituality and Mental Health Care*, 120.
15. Swinton, *Spirituality and Mental Health Care*, 121.

"active wish" ("I want to kill myself"), or a repetitive, obsessive thought "without any volitional quality." Beck and Alford describe the obsessive kind as sometimes manifesting as a form of daydreaming or meticulous planning. They tell how thoughts of suicide build up little by little and then slacken in intensity.[16]

I can relate to Beck and Alford's observations on this topic. For me, even thinking of suicide acted as a vent to release the pain depression caused. I lay awake in bed at night, tossing and turning, and thought of imaginative ways to kill myself. I imagined mechanically designed devices involving levers and pulleys that would act for me and remove from me the responsibility for my death. If there was an afterlife, and I had to provide an account for taking my life, I wanted to absolve myself by being removed as far from the act of suicide as possible. So, even for an unbeliever like me, I still had a fledgling belief system that trapped me, just like Swinton's research participants. Even though I enacted none of these unrealistic and elaborately designed suicide plots, just thinking about them helped vent a little of depression's pain and made things a little more manageable. Oddly, depression seemed to like me thinking this way.

Crucible Experience

The last theme that arose from Swinton's research of Christians who suffered from depression was that their depression experiences acted as catalysts for positive change. Swinton uses the metaphor of a crucible to describe the process through which, for some, depression works as a refiner's fire purifying the sufferer. For instance, one participant told how depression helped him reevaluate his life, priorities, and values. Depression reorientated his outlook and provided him with a more profound sense of purpose and meaning. Another reflected on their depression experience and observed how it deepened their spirituality and provided deeper and more personal insights than they could ever have imagined. One interviewee described how depression led her to reconsider the truths of her Catholic tradition. This sparked a spiritual quest that led her to become a member of another Christian tradition that understood God in a way more conducive to her experiences of depression.[17] These examples from Swinton's study show

---

16. Beck and Alford, *Depression: Causes and Treatments*, 46.
17. Swinton, *Spirituality and Mental Health Care*, 122–25.

that if a person can positively process their depression experiences, then it might enrich their life and bear fruit.

I do not question the validity of depression as a crucible that can enrich a person's life. It is easy to look back on a horrible experience in hindsight and see its value, but it is challenging to be stuck in the middle of that horrendous experience while trying to see it as something enriching. As we know, depression is a whole-body experience affecting every part of life, not least the sufferer's mind and reasoning process. It is an experience typified by intense negative feelings such as meaninglessness, apathy, suicide, abandonment, and deep darkness. So, it seems odd for a sufferer to think of depression as an enriching experience when they are in the throes of such negative feelings and thought processes. For instance, I look back now as a Christian and reflect on my depression experience. I often tell my story to encourage people, and I am authoring this book. So, I could say depression enriched my life. But would I go through it again? No. When depression dominated me with caustic thought patterns that led me to self-harm, did I ever think that these experiences would one day enrich my life? No. My opinion is that when caught in the throes of depression, the prospect of it acting as an enriching crucible is alien and inconsistent with the pathology of the condition. However, we must recall that Swinton's subjects were Christians, and Christianity has a rich theological history with depression, which can help those suffering to process their negative experiences healthily. We will discuss this in a later chapter, but I do not think it is common for people with depression to understand their struggle as a crucible experience.

3

The Bible and Depression

A MAN WITH AN UNCLEAN SPIRIT

After a night of heavy drinking, I sat alone in my apartment room at the end of my bed. The hollowness inside me acted as a massive amplifier, making my senses super-attuned to my surroundings. The tiny drops of condensation on the inside of the windows ran like tears. Outside, the chill night air carried upon it the voices of late-night stragglers. Their joyful shouts and drunken hollers boomed in contrast to the pressure of the bedroom walls pressing in on me. I gulped another mouthful of cheap vodka and cola. Why had creation singled me out to carry this weight? How could I relieve the pain of this nothingness?

A few days earlier, I tried to use an open-shut knife to cut my forearm, but that was a stupid idea. I clenched my teeth and sawed and sawed, but it took ages to break the skin and draw blood. It was not worth the effort. But now I had an idea. I staggered through to the bathroom with one eye closed. Everything swayed. I fumbled among my toiletries until I retrieved what I needed. The four-bladed razor fit snugly in my palm. Not knowing what to expect, I took a few handfuls of toilet paper.

Moments later, I sat on the edge of my bed. I folded the toilet paper with precision and put it to one side. The four-bladed razor was inadequate as it was, so I pushed and pulled here and there against the plastic surround while trying hard not to cut myself. With a little careful manipulation, one thin razor blade broke free from the head of the razor. "The best a man can get." I hope so.

Where should I cut? My face was one choice. One cut on my cheek, and I would have a scar just like Rambo. I held the razor against my skin for a second. I pressed.

No. Cutting my face was not an option. The forearm? I had a few cuts there from when I used my knife a few days ago. I could not do it there again.

I took my arm out of my shirt, revealing a delicate black and white tattoo of a rose with a crucifix dangling from it on my upper arm. Heaven knows why I bothered getting that.

I pressed the razor tenderly against the crucifix, took a breath, and exhaled. With one slow slice, I pulled the blade towards me. Blood oozed out from the cross, along with a sense of euphoria. The pressure, the emptiness, and the blackness escaped from the wound. My skin prickled, and I felt my face flush. "Wow. It healed me! I was free! I had found peace." This sacrilegious act had healed me!

"Healed." Now, that was a peculiar word. It had been years since God had healed my older cousin of cancer at a healing crusade in London. Why did I remember it now?

Mum was on the phone a lot during those wintry November nights in 1996, calling strangers all over Britain and Europe, trying to find out about the healing crusade the American healing evangelist was supposed to be having in London. It had something to do with my cousin Maureen. She and her son, Vardin, lived half an hour away. Maureen was a lot older than me, but Vardin and I were about the same age. Vardin and I grew up together and had many happy memories, but they counted for very little now because cancer was killing his mother, my cousin.

About a month earlier, mum and I traveled to Kirkcaldy to see my cousin while admitted to the Victoria Hospital. My cousin lay scrunched up like a pretzel in the hospital bed in the ward's corner next to an enormous window. Her smile displayed loose narrow teeth, and the warmth in her eyes did nothing to cast away the shadow that loomed over her feeble frame. Her face had a gray-yellow pallor to it, somewhat like the floor. "My, look who it is," she said.

She always said that. From when I was a little boy, I remember her crouching down over me with her hands on her knees and her long black hair cascading over her face. "My look who it is." Her face beamed, and her eyes captured me in a radiance that would make any little child feel like the most precious person in the world.

She tried to push herself up on her bed as Vardin, my mum, and her mother moved passed me to help her. I released the reality of the doorpost and followed them, trying to hide in their wake. Whatever cancer was, it was terrible, and it was killing my cousin.

That evening, we left the hospital and went to a posh hotel. My family always could turn tragedy into feasting.

"You've broken your leg! Okay, let's go to Pizza Hut."

"That was a good reading of the will. Now let's eat."

"Will there be sandwiches after the funeral?"

"Oh, you've got cancer. That's awful. Let's eat."

My cousin's cancer was the reason my mum was on the phone so much. She had no sooner called one person than she was hanging up and punching in the digits to dial her sister Betty, Maureen's mum, explaining what the last call was about. They would confer in their north-of-Scotland accents, and then mum would hang up and begin calling someone else. This went on night after night for about a week.

"That's right." Mum's voice brought me back to reality. She nodded her head, smiled, and laughed to whomever she was speaking to, but I detected a solemnity behind it. "The doctors have only given her a few months."

I listened to the inane chatter between cut scenes in the video game I played. Eventually, mum hung up and looked at me. Her eyes were red. "Do you want to go to London and see Maureen get healed?"

A week later, six of us flew to London and trudged to Wembley Arena for the spectacle. The red buses and black cabs whizzed about us in a swill of drizzle and exhaust fumes. The tall buildings dwarfed us. Being from a tiny fishing village, I had never seen so many people in one place. I saw more people in London in one second than I would see in Pittenweem in a lifetime. It was like visiting a city on a different planet. The sounds, smells, and dizzying amount of movement bombarded the senses. I struggled to take it in. The Londoners, obviously, were unfazed by it all. They walked purposefully around each other, in and out of shops, and expertly negotiated the busy roads, hopping from lane to lane between cars.

With suitcases and rucksacks in tow, the city's energy pulled us along. From walking for miles, to some taxi rides, to walking for miles again, the city's momentum and our mission's expectancy propelled us to Wembley Arena.

Maureen walked hunched over like a half-shut pen knife, pulling her black coat around her chest to hide her discomfort, but I never heard her complain. The excitement and energy of the city pushed her along in the same way it did us.

We arrived at Wembley Arena very early and waited in the foyer. Hundreds of people of all shapes and sizes milled around, waiting for the auditorium to open. The stewards, with their luminescent-yellow bibs, waded through the crowd and entered and exited through doors inaccessible to the public. Sometimes people in the crowd pulled the stewards over from whatever they were doing for a few seconds and asked something of them—probably when the doors would open. Over time, the food kiosks surrounding the auditorium opened their shutters, and those brave enough to leave the lines and risk losing their place joined the food lines. Time took ages to pass. At this rate, my cousin would die before she even got in.

After an eternity, the doors opened, and most of those standing in line rushed forward, fighting each other for the best seats closest to the stage. The crowd showed no compassion and pushed aside older people and pregnant women in the stampede. People scrambled and struggled to get the best seats.

In the middle of this frenzy, we found average seats and had to sit for just as long again before the stage started filling. There were musicians of every kind, a choir, and its conductor. A ministry associate, or someone, came on stage and welcomed everyone before the show started. Then the music began filling the entire auditorium. It came and went in crescendos, caressing the audience in its waves—all except me. I looked at those around me. The same people fighting for the best seats only a few hours before, now sang praises to God and cried with their hands upraised. It was an odd sight.

The music gently waned, and all became still. A little white-suited man came from behind the orchestra. The entire auditorium waited, and the people's anticipation grew until the building was ready to burst. Then, with perfect timing, the man spoke with a peculiar accent. He talked in a slow, soothing manner about God and God's Spirit—whom he was very keen on not upsetting or scaring away. The man flowed in this vein for half an hour, moving between praying, singing, and directing his organist. It was boring. Why had I signed up for this?

As the show neared its climax, the pristine evangelist asked people who needed healing to come forward. They responded in droves and lined up at each side of the stage. Men in suits ushered people on and off the stage, for whom the little evangelist prayed. He waved his hands, blew on the people, and sometimes waved from the other end of the stage. To my surprise, audience members of all shapes and sizes fell on the ground, "slain in the Spirit." Some took a little more "slaying" than others, but most of them fell. One large, smartly-suited man, who must have weighed 300 lbs., was somehow catapulted back over two rows of chairs. Among the bodies, the men in suits trotted around at the evangelist's request, catching people and picking up others.

My mum grabbed one of these suited men during a break between services and spoke to him about my cousin. He looked over to where she stood smoking as my mum told him about her cancer. After a few moments, the man went away. Near the end of the following performance, the suited man approached our seats and invited my cousin and her mom to the stage. The flamboyant evangelist prayed over them, and they fell like the others. And that was that. God healed her of cancer.

Towards the end of that session—it must have been the last performance—the evangelist said, "If any of you want to feel the Holy Spirit, then raise your hands."

This was too good to be true. If any of that stuff happening on stage was true, then I wanted to experience it. I raised my hands.

The evangelist shouted something indistinct, and electricity tingled down my outstretched arms, through my body, and to my feet. My heart raced, but I felt oddly calm and at peace as if I breathed for the first time. How on earth could that evangelist wave his hands like that and make all of us feel God? No wonder everyone had been fighting to get the seats close to the stage if this is what he could dish out. But what was the evangelist saying now? He mentioned something about how the blood of Jesus brings healing and about the blood running down from the cross.

The bright red blood ran down from the cross on the tattoo of my arm to the bedsheets. Damn! I threw the bloody razor onto the bedside table, grabbed the white toilet paper, and blotted the cut. The darkness returned with each blot. Freedom was fleeting, and despair returned. What was I to do? The answer looked obvious.

I picked up the razor from the bedside table. It slipped against my fingers, smearing my index finger and thumb in blood. Without a second thought, I cut again—this time going in the opposite direction across the crucifix, forming an X shape.

Blood oozed out from both axes like a teacher's red mark for a wrong answer on an exam paper. The crucifix tattoo was wrong. God did not exist.

And if he did exist, I wanted him to know how I felt. I wanted him to know what I thought of everything that his cross represented. I wanted him to know that I detested him. But neither such feelings nor the cutting made the pain go away. It always returned.

Looking back at this, and my many other self-harming experiences, I often wonder if the demon-possessed man in the Gospel of Mark experienced the same (Mark 5:1–20). He lived among the tombs in such a physical and psychological state that he broke the chains that bound him. Although typically used only on criminals, maybe his community chained him up as an act of care and love on behalf of his friends and family who wanted to protect him from himself. Perhaps the chains in the story could be an analogy for the way we use antidepressant medicine. Nevertheless, nothing could bind him. Night and day among the tombs and on the mountains, he cried out and cut himself with stones.

I assume that we experienced the same thing. My life was off the rails. Nothing could restrain me or help me fight against the monstrous darkness that overpowered me. It was a part of my life. Like the man from the Gospel of Mark, the day turned into night and night turned into day. Unclean places were my refuge, and, as if I lived in the mountains, isolation was my home. Relief came from cutting myself. One may say that self-harming was my call for help. To me, cutting was the only thing that made the pain go away. Others may not see it, and I certainly did not see it at the time, but the man in the Gospel of Mark was me.

IS DEPRESSION IN THE BIBLE?

The demon-possessed man in the Gospel of Mark, or the Gerasene Demoniac as he is often known, shows that self-harm is in the Bible. Nonetheless, a specific word for depression in either the Greek or Hebrew language is absent from the biblical text. Still, depression is a condition that has afflicted humanity since ancient times. It is clear from the Old Testament that ancient societies were well aware of mental disorders, which John Wilkinson says shows that depression is not just a recent complaint, but is a condition that has afflicted humankind since ancient times.[1] The ancients did not understand depression the way we do today, but that does not mean their experiences of hopelessness, apathy, and meaningless were that much different from ours.

---

1. Wilkinson, *The Bible and Healing*, 150.

In his work, Paul Kruger compiled several methods from scholars of ancient Near Eastern literature to identify depression in the Bible. This is useful to help us detect depression and to see its effects throughout the Bible.

1. The first method identifies depressive symptoms within the ancient literature that concur with those symptoms in the *Diagnostic and Statistical Manual of Mental Disorders* (DSM). Healthcare professionals use the DSM as a tool to diagnose mental illnesses. In this method, researchers study the Bible and use the DSM's diagnostic criteria to discover and substantiate mental health condition.
2. A second method uses specific body postures and movements to identify depression within the biblical text.
3. A third method classifies eating, sleeping, and other disturbances within the Bible to identify depressio.
4. A fourth method identifies depression by focusing on those texts that present a negative outlook on life and dwell on death thoughts.[2]

The prophet Elijah provides one Old Testament example of these methodologies at work. After meeting Ahab, Elijah went up Mount Carmel and "bowed down on the ground and put his face between his knees" (1 Kgs 18:42). Assuming a downward posture such as bowing might reveal depression. First Kings 19:6–7 describes how an angel came to Elijah and compelled him to eat. According to the methods, Elijah's lack of appetite is synonymous with the physical symptoms of depression. In the same passage, verse 4 tells how Elijah prayed to die. Again, Elijah's actions hint at depressive behavior. Ahab is another figure that emerges from the Old Testament as one possibly suffering from depression. The Bible describes how he "went into his house sullen and displeased because of the word which Naboth the Jezreelite had spoken to him. . . . And he lay down on his bed, and turned away his face, and would eat no food" (1 Kgs 21:4). Other examples are Job, Jeremiah (Jer 20:14–15), and Jonah (Jonah 4:3).

Mathew S. Stanford provides another example of depression in the Bible through his study on King David. He created the table below to show how King David's self-expressions, as journaled in the Psalms, are the same as those expressed by depression sufferers today. King David lived in c.1000 B.C. Despite his incredible achievements and being called a man after God's

---

2. Kruger, "Depression in the Hebrew Bible," 188–98.

own heart (1 Sam 3:14), David had issues in his personal life and knew great sorrow. One such experience Stanford discusses is in 2 Samuel 11. This Bible chapter focuses on David's relationship with Bathsheba, and Stanford says that David's behavior in this chapter shows depression symptoms. The fact David is not present leading the army may show occupational impairment (v. 1), which is a sign of depression. His sleeplessness (v. 2) may also be a symptom. David also seems unable to make rational decisions. Sleeping with a married woman and murdering her husband are two examples of David's poor decision-making. Later in 2 Samuel 13:21 (18:5; 19:1–7; 1 Kgs 1:6), three of David's sons break family and relational boundaries, and in Stanford's words, "the Scriptures describe David as being emotionally paralyzed and unable to discipline or correct them." The fact David seems impaired in his ability to interact and relate to others in the way expected of someone in his position further shows that David may have suffered from depression.[3]

David's impairment corresponds to Jay Adams' understanding. He suggests that depression comes when someone mishandles a situation or any number of situations. The person's mishandling then begins a downward spiral into depression. Adams says, "The downward cycle of sin moves from a problem to a faulty, sinful response, thereby causing an additional complicating problem which is met by additional sinful responses, etc."[4]

---

3. Stanford, *Grace for the Afflicted*, 54–56.
4. Adams, *The Christian Counselor's Manual*, 375–76.

Biblical Examples of Major Depressive Disorder[5]

Characteristic Symptoms	David's Symptoms	Reference
Depressed mood	Mourning/sorrow all day, weeping.	Psalm 6:6–7; 13:2; 31:10;
Significant weight loss or decrease in appetite	Forgets to eat, bones cling to the flesh, weak from fasting.	Psalm 102:4–5; 109:24
Insomnia	Crying all night, no rest at night, could not sleep.	Psalm 6:6; 22:2; 102:7; 2 Samuel 11:2
Psychomotor retardation	He feels like a deaf and dumb man. He experiences fear and trembling.	Psalm 38:13–14; 55:5
Fatigue or loss of energy	His strength dried up/fails. His vitality drained away. His heart has withered away.	Psalm 22:14–15; 31:10; 32:4; 38:10; 102:4
Feelings of worthlessness	He describes himself as a worm—not a man—and a reproach to others: "No one cares for my soul."	Psalm 22:6; 31:12–13; 69:12; 109:25; 142:4
Diminished ability to think or concentrate, or indecisiveness	He did not go to war and was unable to discipline his rebellious son.	2 Samuel 11:1; 13:21; 18:5; 19:1–7; 1 Kings 1:6
Recurrent thoughts of death	He describes terrors of death.	Psalm 22:15; 55:4

The above examples show that although the Bible does not directly reference depression, its symptoms are evident within its pages. However, we need to be careful, because medical anthropology is increasingly showing that medicocentric views of disease are incompatible with historical biblical interpretation. A medicocentric view of disease is used by interpreters to give a modern western scientific explanation of what the Bible characters experienced as illness. For example, some medicocentric views say that King Saul had bipolar disorder. Others say that Saul most likely suffered from depression initially brought on by PTSD. Still others say that Saul's ecstatic spiritual experiences suggest epilepsy, perhaps caused by a brain tumor.[6] However, John Pilch says we must be careful of such biomedically

---

5. Stanford, *Grace for the Afflicted*, 55. Adapted by the author.
6. For some discussion into Saul's illness, see Ben-Noun, Liubov (Louba), "What Was the Mental Disease That Afflicted King Saul?," *Clinical Case Studies* 2 (October, 2003)

infused western interpretations because it is impossible to know for sure what the biblical characters experienced. Therefore, any interpretation as to what the biblical figures actually suffered from is, for the most part, hypothetical. Pilch writes, "In the end, as cross-culturally sensitive researchers readily admit, a modern reader simply does not and cannot know what the health problem might have been, or whether or not it was even physical."[7] Despite Pilch's observations, having a method in mind helps us interact with and learn from those people in the Bible whose experiences appear similar to our present-day experiences of depression.

THE BIBLICAL CAUSES OF DEPRESSION

Sin's Role in Creation

Although the examples mentioned above reveal some Bible figures experienced something similar to depression, they do not provide any insight into what the Bible says might actually cause depression. Exploring this question requires we place depression within the broader context of mental health and disease.

In the first chapter, we discussed how depression is a disease (i.e., a biological dysfunction causing health's absence), an illness (i.e., it has personal meaning known only to the sufferer), and a sickness (i.e., it carries a social label). In doing this, we showed depression's extensiveness and the extent to which it weaves into every part of the sufferer's life. Seeing depression in this capacity further helps us consider its holistic dynamic as a disruption of biological, personal, and social relationships. Thinking about depression by using the analogy of relationships unites it with sin's presence in creation along with the alienation and division that sin has caused and continues to produce.

In the Book of Genesis, God formed Adam from the dust of the ground and breathed life into his nostrils (Gen 2:7). John Levision describes how with this intimate act, what was once lifeless soil became an "affirmation of life, the quintessence of creation, and the core of human vitality.[8] Levison continues to note how the life of God's breath clashed with the emptiness of

---

270–82; Gillian P. Williams and Magdel le Roux, "King Saul's Mysterious Malady." *HTS Teologiese Studies/Theological Studies* 68 (January, 2012) 1–6.

7. Pilch, "Disease.

8. Levison, *Filled With the Spirit*, 15.

the dirt, filling it with energy to bring the dead to life.[9] Thus, there are two elements present, the dead dirt and the infusion of life. Both of these provide a remarkable description of our beginning on earth. However, what started so beautifully ended in disaster. Adam and Eve ate of the fruit of the forbidden tree, which opened their eyes to know good and evil. Their disobedience forced God to intervene to prevent them from eating from the Tree of Life, thereby living forever in a perpetual state of sin (Gen 3:22). God judged the event according to his righteous standard and perfect ability. Because his judgments are always righteous, true, and perfectly suited to the occasion in which he judges, his decree is no more and no less than what the situation warranted.

> To the woman He said:
> "I will greatly multiply your sorrow and your conception;
> In pain you shall bring forth children;
> Your desire shall be for your husband,
> And he shall rule over you."
> Then to Adam He said, "Because you have heeded the voice of your wife, and have eaten from the tree of which I commanded you, saying, 'You shall not eat of it':
> "Cursed is the ground for your sake;
> In toil you shall eat of it
> All the days of your life.
> Both thorns and thistles it shall bring forth for you,
> And you shall eat the herb of the field.
> In the sweat of your face you shall eat bread
> Till you return to the ground,
> For out of it you were taken;
> For dust you are,
> And to dust you shall return."
> (Gen 3:16–19)

God cursed the dirt from which he formed Adam and into which he breathed life. So now, at the end of Adam's lifecycle, Adam's life-breath will return to God, and his body will return to the ground (v. 19). Death now surrounds and infuses Adam's life to the extent that he now toils the cursed land to eat its fruit (vv. 17–18).

The fact that God cursed the ground shows the curse's extensiveness: the entire creation now suffers death's effects. The curse even affects the entrance of new life into creation, for in the same way that Adam will bring

---

9. Levison, *Filled With the Spirit*, 15.

forth the earth's fruit with toil, Eve will bring forth the fruit of childbirth in pain (v. 16). Not only this, but an unequal relationship system will bring its own tensions, typifying Eve's relationship with her husband (v. 16). Through their actions, Adam and Eve forced God into a position where he responded by allowing humanity to thrive within the "walls of mortality."[10] Their actions have unimaginable ramifications for the entire creation.

Adam and Eve's disobedience distorted God's original perfect creation with far-reaching consequences that subjected all creation to death, decay, and degeneration.[11] Sin entered creation and disrupted relationships within families, communities, nations, and the rest of the created order.[12] Robin Cover comments on how the Jews viewed sin like many of their Middle Eastern counterparts as a "universal moral flaw, pandemic in the human race."[13] Their extensive understanding meant they thought sin disrupted relationships and caused alienation inside and outside the body, even causing disease.[14]

The understanding that disrupted relationships cause diseases is not too far removed from our current medical view of healing. It also understands that relationship disruption causes disease, but only in the much narrower biological sense in which organs, cells, nerves, etc., make up the human body and live in harmony with each other. If something unbalances the relationships in this complex system, then disease (i.e., a biological abnormality or dysfunction) will occur. Therefore, the medical model believes that healing comes through "the restoration of the homeostatic relationships of the patient as an individual organism."[15] On the contrary, in connection to their broader view of sin's disruption of relationships in creation, the people of the ancient world approached healing by realigning themselves with the cosmos and their god(s), which took place through religious ritual practice. For the Old Testament Hebrews, relationship realignment took place through the ritual enactment of the Levitical practices. Thus, according to the people of the Bible, healing was a religious act that comprised relationship restoration with oneself, one's family, one's

---

10. Levison, *Filled With the Spirit*, 24.
11. White, *The Masks of Melancholy*, 23.
12. McDougal, "Sin," 473.
13. Cover, "Sin, Old Testament," 32.
14. Sulmasy, "A Biopsychosocial-Spiritual Model," 25.
15. Sulmasy, "A Biopsychosocial-Spiritual Model," 26.

community, and one's God.¹⁶ The ultimate restoration of these relationships comes through Jesus Christ's atoning work, which delivers us from sin and restores our relationship with God (Rom 5:1; Eph 2:14–18; Col 1:20), our relationships with each other (Mark 9:50; Rom 12:18; 14:19; 1 Cor 7:15; 2 Cor 13:11; 1 Thess 5:13), and our relationships with ourselves. The result of these restored relationships is peace.¹⁷

We need to realize, though, that although Christ has redeemed us, and we are new creations empowered by the Spirit, we still live within the tension of the "already but not yet." Degeneration, disease, and death became part of the human experience because of the fall and sin's entrance into the world. Being in the world, Christians are not yet entirely free from the effects of sin, including disease and death. The Bible describes how we groan inwardly waiting for our new glorified bodies that will be free from the weaknesses of fallen creation (Rom 8:22–23), which we will receive when the dead in Christ rise (1 Cor 15:42–44, 51–54). In the meantime, sin affects humankind directly and indirectly.

How Sin, Directly and Indirectly, Causes Disease and Depression

John White provides an example of sin affecting someone indirectly. He describes a lady, called Aunt Mary, who has rheumatism. White says that her rheumatism was not caused by any direct sin on her part, although it could be in some cases. In her case, though, the only thing that caused her condition was that she was born into a creation where decay and degeneration are normal. She has rheumatism, then, for no other reason than she is human and is getting older. Alternatively, sin can also cause disease directly. Substance abuse is one example White provides. For instance, if substance abuse is a sin, then one may easily consider an alcoholic's liver condition as a disease resulting directly from their sin. Another example White provides is of someone committing adultery. Should the adulterer contract an STD, then the disease is a direct result of their sin. Not only that, but the broken relationships caused by their infidelity are also direct results.¹⁸

I am sure that some would oppose these examples of sin directly causing disease by arguing that conditions in the alcoholic's or the adulterer's life might have conditioned them to be predisposed to these addictions and

---

16. Sulmasy, "A Biopsychosocial-Spiritual Model," 25
17. Wilkinson, *The Bible and Healing*, 23.
18. White, *Masks of Melancholy*, 23.

actions. Therefore, they are no more responsible for their kidney disorder, their STD, or the broken relationships caused by their infidelity, than Aunt Mary is responsible for her rheumatism. As interesting as individual case studies involving the extent to which people are accountable for their own actions might be, it is not my aim to argue one way or the other. Instead, I provide these examples to get our minds thinking about how creation's subjection to degeneration may affect our lives. Even then, there are biblical examples of sin causing disease directly and indirectly.

A biblical example of sin directly causing sickness might be the lame man at the Pool of Bethesda in John 5:1–15. "After healing him, Jesus said, 'See, you have been made well. Sin no more, lest a worse thing come upon you'" (v. 14). Jesus' words reveal that personal sin caused the man's disease and continued sin would result in more bad things happening to him. Similarly, James 5:13–16 speaks about healing in the context of prayer and repentance. Regarding this, Scot McKnight describes how the ancient world saw sickness as more of a mystery than we consider it today I assume this is because they did not have our medical knowledge. McKnight explains that ancient communities sought to resolve this mystery by connecting sickness to sin. Within this sickness and sin dynamic, there are many New Testament examples in which repentance is the logical solution for illness. For example, Jesus healed a paralyzed man and said, "Son, your sins are forgiven," implying that the paralysis was the result of sin (Mark 2:5; cf. John 5:14). Paul also mentions people in the Corinthian church who were sick because of sin (1 Cor 11:30).[19] Therefore, the Bible seems to make a secure connection between a sick person's illness and the direct consequences of sin.

One Bible passage that further enriches our understanding of illness in the Bible is John 9:2–3. This passage describes how Jesus healed a man who was born blind. It reads, "Now as Jesus passed by, He saw a man who was blind from birth. And His disciples asked Him, saying, 'Rabbi, who sinned, this man or his parents, that he was born blind?' Jesus answered, 'Neither this man nor his parents sinned, but that the works of God should be revealed in him.'" Jesus' answer to the disciples' question moves the disciples' attention away from sin and toward the larger narrative of Jesus' redemptive role in creation. One key feature of the redemptive story is that Christ is the second Adam. The first Adam's disobedience led to sin and death for all, but the second Adam's obedience leads to righteous and

---

19. McKnight, *The Letter of James*, 218–19.

abundant life for everyone (Rom 5:12–21). However, although Jesus corrected his disciples when they suggested that the blind man's parents' sin caused his disability, Jesus never discredited their idea. According to Craig Keener, those living in the ancient world believed that the consequences of parental sin could pass to their children and manifest through disease and disability (cf. Exod 20:5).[20]

Even today this idea is not too far-fetched. People's sinful actions do have consequences in the lives of others. For instance, a consensus exists that links the development of depression in children with childhood trauma.[21] Studies show that childhood emotional and sexual abuse substantially affect the severity of symptoms in chronically depressed adults.[22] In her article on child abuse and depression, Ellen McGrath writes, "In almost every case of significant adult depression, the depressive experienced some form of abuse in childhood, either physical, sexual, emotional or, often, a combination."[23] These studies reveal that the disciples' question was not unfounded. In such cases, we see how sin directly causes illness and that there is a link between the sinful behavior of one and the illness of another. In the case of the blind man in John 9, Jesus may have moved the disciples' focus away from sin as the cause of the man's blindness towards Jesus' redemptive role, but he never said that someone's sin could not affect another person. The fact is our actions have consequences for others as well as for ourselves.

Daniel 4 tells the story of King Nebuchadnezzar and provides another example of sin directly causing illness—apparently some kind of mental illness in this case. William B. Nelson sees Nebuchadnezzar's story as representing an actual metamorphic transformation from human to beast, rather than an illness like lycanthropy or zoanthropy, or some other form of insanity.[24] White, on the other hand, although hesitant to suggest a diagnosis, is sure that Nebuchadnezzar's transformation was metaphorical and representative of some form of mental illness that made him act like a wild animal.[25] Samuel Wells and George Sumner suggest lycanthropy.[26] These opinions aside, what is striking about Nebuchadnezzar's mental

---

20. Keener, *The Gospel of John*, 777–78.
21. Negele et al., "Childhood Trauma."
22. Negele et al., "Childhood Trauma."
23. McGrath, "Child Abuse and Depression."
24. Nelson, *Daniel*, 130–31, 139.
25. White, *Masks of Melancholy*, 24–25.
26. Wells and Sumner, *Esther and Daniel*, 148.

illness is that it resulted from God's chastisement. The Bible explains how Nebuchadnezzar had an awful dream in which he saw himself driven out of society and living like a wild animal. Daniel interpreted the dream and explained it was prophetic. He advised Nebuchadnezzar to stop sinning and break from his wicked past (Dan 4:27). In other words, Daniel urged Nebuchadnezzar to repent. Because Nebuchadnezzar did not repent, his dream came to pass twelve months later. His restoration began at God's appointed time when "I, Nebuchadnezzar, looked up to heaven. My sanity returned, and I praised and worshiped the Most High and honored the one who lives forever" (v. 34). This example shows how sin, specifically pride, directly caused Nebuchadnezzar's condition. As White says, Nebuchadnezzar's story affirms that a wrong relationship with God can expose a person to mental illness, and that a right relationship with God is a step toward mental health.[27]

Demons Causing Disease and Depression

One thing that is striking in the Nebuchadnezzar narrative is the absence of demons or other spirits as the cause of his mental illness. Contemporary opinion regularly assumes that ancient societies saw demons as the go-to explanation for the cause of mental illness.[28] Even today, many Christians place a strong emphasis on the role of demons in mental illness.[29] This assumption is justifiable considering the many New Testament examples of demons causing physical and psychological problems. The Gerasene Demoniac is one example (Mark 5:1–20), and the lady in the synagogue with the bad back is another (Luke 13:10–17). Still, the Bible does not mention demons in the Nebuchadnezzar narrative.

Mental illness also plays a role in 1 Samuel 21:10–15, but there is no mention of demons in the text either. This passage describes how David fled from King Saul and went to King Achish of the Philistine city of Gath. The Israelites and the Philistines were enemies, so King Achish's officers were unhappy with David being there. They spoke to King Achish and reminded him of David's past military exploits and how, until recently, David had been their enemy and that King Achish could not trust David. Fear gripped David when he heard these comments. Unsure how King Achish would

---

27. White, *Masks of Melancholy*, 25.
28. Nemade et al., "Historical Understandings of Depression."
29. White, *Masks of Melancholy*, 29.

react, David pretended to be insane by scratching on doors and drooling down his beard (1 Sam 21:12–14). King Achish responded and said to his men, "Must you bring me a madman? We already have enough of them around here! Why should I let someone like this be my guest?" (1 Sam 21:12–15 NLT).

It is interesting to note that both David and King Achish had pictures in their minds of what mental illness and insanity looked like in a person. David's acting skills must have been compelling because King Achish did not doubt David's madness. No doubt, David's firsthand experience with King Saul's bouts of insanity equipped David well. Nevertheless, neither King Achish nor his staff mentions demons when they see an insane David before them. In comparison, the Bible clearly states that an evil spirit caused King Saul's mental health problems (1 Sam 16:14–23; 19:8–10). White concludes that ancient societies must have understood that sometimes demons caused mental illness and sometimes they did not.[30]

The account of the Gerasene Demoniac (Mark 5:1–20) is one example of a demon causing mental health issues. The passage describes how, night and day, this man was in the mountains and the tombs, crying out and cutting himself with stones. His behavior is consistent with mental illness,[31] and the fact Jesus healed the man by casting out the demons shows that demons caused it.

An opposite account that dismisses demons causing mental health issues is in Acts 12:1–19. In this passage, an angel helped Peter escape from prison. Peter returned to Mary's house and knocked on the door. When Rhoda came to answer it and saw Peter outside, she ran back into the house in disbelief and told the others that Peter was there. They responded, "Thou art mad" (v. 15 KJV). The Greek word (*mainŏmai*) translated as "mad" means precisely that. They thought Rhoda was mad in much the same way that we would glibly call a close friend crazy for having a zany idea. However, the New Testament only uses the Greek word they called her by (*mainŏmai*) five times (John 10:20; Acts 12:15; 26:24, 25; 1 Cor 14:23), and only in John 19:20 is the word connected with demons and demon-affliction.[32] The word *mainŏmai* has no demonic connection

---

30. White, *Masks of Melancholy*, 26.
31. Guth, "An Insider's Look at the Gerasene Disciple (Mark 5:1–20), 61–70. Guth interviewed people with mental illness to gather their perspectives on the story of the Gerasene Demoniac. Her study showed significant points of identification with her subjects' experiences and the demoniac's.
32. Mounce, "Μαίνομαι."

in the four other cases. White comments, "However, crazy Rhoda might have seemed, her brothers and sisters would hardly have accused her of *that* [being demonized]."[33] Also, in Mark 3:21 and Acts 26:24, both Jesus' and Paul's opponents accuse them of being mad and do not reference demons. Elsewhere, though, opponents do claim Jesus' power came from demons (Matt 12:22–30; Mark 3:20–27). Overall, White argues that people living in the Old and New Testament times saw "unusual mental states" resulting from both natural sources (i.e., madness) and from demons. As White says, the trick is knowing when to connect the cause of an illness to demons or to natural occurrences. However, as it stands, it seems that it was easier for those who wrote the Bible to differentiate between the two than it is for contemporary Christians to differentiate. As White says, "We are better talking about demons than at spotting or dealing with them."[34]

HOW THE BIBLE CAN HELP DEPRESSION SUFFERERS

The Bible has much to say about depression, mental health, and disease in general. Our society and the church may need encouragement to talk about mental illness and depression, but the Bible is not quiet about the problem. It provides us with many examples upon which to ponder. Still, it would be nice if the Bible specified the cause of mental illness and other diseases, but other than showing sin as the root of the issue, the Bible gives no definitive explanation. Nevertheless, even if the Bible does not give us all the information we seek, it offers the solution. In my survey that accompanied my doctoral research, I discovered that a large proportion of respondents found the Bible helpful in their battle with depression. Forty-six percent of people either "strongly agreed" or "agreed" that the Bible was useful, and a further 25 percent saw the local church and the Bible as mutually beneficial. This means that 71 percent of the respondents felt there was a benefit in using the Bible.[35] This reflects what Stanford observed in his research about how King David expressed his feelings and found relief in God through psalm-writing. It is worth quoting Stanford in full:

> There is an important lesson to be learned from this biblical example of depression. In a time before psychological and psychiatric

---

33. White, *Masks of Melancholy*, 26–27.
34. White, *Masks of Melancholy*, 26–27.
35. McBain, "Exploring the Silent Nature of Depression," 153.

treatments existed, David found relief from his suffering in God's unchanging character, infinite faithfulness, and unconditional love. David took his sorrow and pain to God, and there he found a foundation of hope from which he could rebuild. Hope that transcends our circumstances, even depression, is only available in the loving God who created us, sustains us, and made a way for us to be in an eternal relationship with him. David knew this truth well, and he tightly held to it throughout his life. Our first response in times of mental distress should be to seek God. Finding our hope in him is the first step on the journey to recovery.[36]

Swinton speaks about the benefits of liturgy and worship in helping sufferers find meaning and hope in the midst of depression. He notes that the Psalms were particularly useful in assisting sufferers in expressing their feelings when their intellect could not comprehend what exactly they were experiencing. Describing how one of his research participants used the Psalms, Swinton says, "When she did not have words to express her agony, she allows these simple words to become a vehicle for the expression of her psychological pain and the deep spiritual need."[37]

Swinton explains how people use the Psalms in a personal and relational manner, through which they reflect on the psalmist's experiences while considering their own experiences. The reader travels through the turmoil with the psalmist to a place of renewed faith and trust in God's stability. "In this way, the Bible provides the language that formulates the boundaries within which one understands and expresses their experiences of depression."[38] This relational reading of the scriptures provides those who are struggling with depression the certainty that God is with them throughout their experiences. Using the Bible to combat depression, especially using the Psalms, is meaningful to me. I will not go into too much detail here, but the Psalms acted as a lens and an outlet through which I could reflect on my experiences and communicate them to God.

---

36. Stanford, *Grace for the Afflicted*, 57.
37. Swinton, *Spirituality and Mental Health Care*, 129.
38. Swinton, *Spirituality and Mental Health Care*, 130–31.

4

Rescued but not Resuscitated

PEACEFULLY SUFFOCATING

It was December in Aberdeen, Scotland. The silver granite buildings shone, and the black roads sparkled with frost. It had been like that throughout the day too, but now that it was nighttime, the moon's glow made the buildings and the streets sparkle in a way that made them seem extra hard and brittle.

I had been out all night drinking with my friends and had a skinful. It was just like any other night, filled with drinking, laughter, and music, as we hit one bar after another until the last bar closed, and then we ended up on Belmont Street. Inebriated and disheveled adults packed the street, looking for lost drunken friends, hooking up with strangers, and getting takeout. Immaculately dressed at the beginning of the night, they now looked like extras out of the movie *Night of the Living Dead*. They staggered around with their fast food in their hands, being sick on street corners, and peeing down alleyways.

After buying a kebab or something from a takeout, I hung around with the other zombies until Belmont Street steadily emptied, then I staggered back to my apartment alone. There was nothing in my mind, but an idea came to me as I got to my apartment door. The salty fragrance of the sea wafting from the harbor along with the imaginary sound of the waves rolling against the shore inspired my idea. Everything at that moment seemed so logical, and I knew what I had to do and where I had to go.

My stroll to the beach took me away from the city center's bars and nightclubs, and away from the gaudy glow of the culturally inoffensive Christmas lights. "Bah! Humbug!" The shouts of late-night revelers diminished against the silence of the night, and the warmth of the yellow streetlights faded against the icy calm North Sea and the white sand. Everything sparkled. The moon twinkled and danced upon the face of the waters.

Years before, I read *The Perfect Storm* by Sebastian Junger. What I remember most about that book was the way he described drowning. If I recalled correctly, he said it was like peacefully suffocating. That did not sound like such a terrible way to go.

I tossed my jacket aside and tiptoed up to the water's edge. All I had to do was take one step, then another, then another, and soon it would all be over. The water would embrace me, and there would be no more pain. "Peacefully suffocating." It didn't sound like such a terrible way to go. Drowning could not be worse than staying here and living.

I took the first step. The water crept through the leather of my boots. "It's kind of warm." I expected it to be ice cold.

A second step, and it came above my ankles. The lower part of my jeans clung uncomfortably to my calves. "This is easier than I thought."

Another mechanical step, and the water came up to my knees. Then another step and another step. The water submerged my waist. I shivered. Now it was getting colder.

A few more brave steps and I would reach the point of no return, and then the pain would come, followed by peace. All I had to do was keep walking to that point then it would be too late even if I did change my mind. The sea would make my decision for me and absolve me from any responsibility for taking my own life.

My jeans rubbed against my thighs as I took the next step. The sea's rhythmical swelling and abating seemed more significant now that the water reached my chest. Everything—the moon and the stars—seemed so high up, as if I looked up from the bottom of a deep well. They welcomed me into their embrace.

I seemed to float. That was not part of the plan! I was supposed to drown, not float! Maybe I should start swimming out into the darkness?

A buzzing noise came from back on the beach. It was my phone ringing. I could not remember calling anyone before I entered the water, so there was no reason at all for anyone to call this late.

For some odd reason, I waded out of the water and answered the phone. To this day, I am not sure who it was or if it was anyone at all. All I know is that it broke the spell and stopped me from doing what I planned.

I stood wet and cold on the beach, with only the moon and the sea as witnesses to what has just happened. "So that was that. So close, and yet so far."

A chill ran over me. Boy, it was cold. The sea was much warmer and pleasant than the frosty air. And my jeans! My jeans felt like sandpaper against the inside of my legs, and they rubbed me raw as I walked home with my boots squelching. Rub, squelch, rub, squelch, rub, squelch. I walked the empty streets as if I had soiled myself.

Who knew what the clerk at the service station thought when I tossed him a drenched bill. "A twenty pack of cigarettes and a lighter, please." I assumed he had seen worse. One thing was for sure: he would not have seen me at all if the situation with the phone had not happened. I would have been with Robert Taylor.

Somehow my mother found out about this event. It was maybe my sister who called on the beach. I genuinely cannot remember. Anyway, my mother found out. She called the doctor, and he said I had to come and see him.

I kicked up a fuss. Why would I want to go see the doctor? There was nothing wrong with me! That was the gist of my argument. It seems funny looking back now. I had just tried to commit suicide and had been self-harming, yet I thought there was nothing wrong with me. Anyway, after a lot of kickback from me, they convinced me to go. The general threat was that if I did not see the doctor, then he would send someone to come and get me. I envisioned men with white coats hauling me out of my apartment and putting me in a white van. I did not know how genuine their threat was, but with my boots still damp, I walked the 30 minutes to the doctor late one evening to attend an emergency appointment.

The doctor explained everything. He told me I was suffering from depression caused by a chemical imbalance in my brain. For all those years, then, every one of those negative thoughts and actions—thoughts of suicide, self-harm, the self-destructive lifestyle—a chemical imbalance in my brain caused them all. The diagnosis seemed logical enough. However, it was odd how easily he attributed my negative behavior to a biochemical imbalance, but he did not consider how the same chemical imbalance might have caused healthy behaviors. For instance, although the depression caused thoughts of hopelessness and despair, I expressed these feelings through poetry, creative writing, and keeping a journal; not once did the doctor consider that the chemical imbalance caused these healthy outlets.

Speaking to the doctor was kind of an anti-climax. I am sure he did not mean it, but he explained away my entire identity and life experience as resulting from nothing more than a series of biochemical impulses in my brain. He reduced my whole life to something over which I had no control. It seemed logical to me, though, that if a biochemical imbalance caused the depression and its associated experiences and behaviors, then the chemicals resident in the prescribed antidepressants would fix my brain, correct the chemical levels, and allow me to behave and think like a normal person.

I put my faith in the medication and took it as prescribed, but it never worked as well as I hoped. The medication was like putting a fresh coat of plaster over a crumbling wall or freshly painting rotten wood. I could easily draw a parallel between the medication and the Gerasene Demoniac's chains. Like the chains, the medication's goal was to help me and stop me from hurting myself, but they were ineffective and kept breaking. The medication did nothing to contain what was inherently wrong on the inside of me.

Every time I returned to the doctor for my check-ups, he responded by increasing the dosage. I would need to use prescriptions, and any other form of medical intervention that the doctor saw fit, to manage this condition for the rest of my life. I hate to say it, but the only thing that eased the mental anguish for a few seconds was cutting myself. The alcohol always helped to numb everything. It was just a pity the doctor could not have prescribed self-harm or another form of bloodletting because that worked a treat. At least the sleeping pills the doctor prescribed worked.

THE BIOMEDICAL MODEL OF HEALTH

The *Diagnostic and Statistical Manual of Mental Disorders* is now in its fifth edition (DSM-5). This is a manual published by the American Psychiatric Association (APA), which lists different mental disorders in order to give medical practitioners a universal language and standard for mental disorder classifications. Under the section on "Depressive Disorders," the DSM-5 contains seven unique kinds of disorders, each type with similar symptoms. What differs among them are issues of duration, timing, or the recognized causes.[1] Emily Durbin explains that healthcare professionals presume someone has depression if their diagnosis includes the signs and symptoms described in DSM-5. This system's significant advantage is that the types and categories the DSM describes provide healthcare professionals with criteria to help with their clinical decisions. Still, there are disadvantages in the way that some signs and symptoms may be common to unique kinds of mental health problems, and that different people may experience the same illness in unique ways. Thus, diagnosis requires the healthcare professional to build up a picture of the patient's mental state before he or she began experiencing the symptoms in order to understand the patient's normal mood level. Once they determine a normal level, the healthcare professional seeks to define the symptoms according to the DSM and determine the extent to which the symptoms deviate from the patient's normal functioning.[2] My doctor used this same approach to diagnose me. He asked calculated questions about what I was like in the past to establish my normal baseline, and then he asked questions about my condition to determine my symptoms. He then assessed my responses and diagnosed me. However, behind this approach sits a broader ideology that dramatically affects how our culture and healthcare professionals understand diseases. The ideology I am referring to is the biomedical model.

The biomedical model of health and medicine developed over the last few hundred years as the dominant model for understanding health and disease. Science is at its foundation, so the biomedical model sits upon empirical claims that the natural world is the only reality.[3] Therefore, our reality consists of only those things that are scientifically verifiable. The model does not consider any societal, psychological, behavioral, and/or spiritual alternatives that may account for the causes of diseases. The biomedical model understands the complexity of any disease by breaking it down to its individual biochemical parts and then exploring the causal relationship between those parts and the disease. It assumes it can fully account for a disease through biological (somatic) deviations in the human body from what it considers as normal.[4] For the biomedical model, a disease is an abnormal deviation in a person's biochemical processes that healthcare professionals must address separately from non-somatic issues.

---

1. American Psychiatric Association, *DSM-5*, 155.
2. Durbin, *Depression 101*, 5–6.
3. Peters, *Science, Theology and Ethics*, 16.
4. Engel, "The Need for a New Medical Model," 39–40.

DEPRESSION, WHERE IS YOUR STING?

With mental diseases like depression, the biomedical model conceptualizes non-somatic issues as the results of underlying biological problems.[5]

As we might expect, in my case, the doctor's approach did not consider any social, psychological, behavioral, or other stressors as the principal cause of my depression. He may have considered these stressors as factors compounding my depression, but, they were not the direct cause, because according to the biomedical model, the immediate cause of depression is always biological. My doctor asked questions about my social life, upbringing, lifestyle, and the rest, but he only used my responses to determine a baseline so that he could understand what normal functioning was for me. After establishing this baseline and checking off my symptoms as I tried to describe what I experienced, the doctor diagnosed depression. He used the biomedical model's reductionist principles to reduce all the feelings, experiences, and thoughts I had to a biochemical imbalance in my brain. The solution to this was to use a drug to fix the chemical imbalance and to bring back to normal the elements of my life negatively affected by the chemical imbalance. I do not want to sound overly critical, but my doctor approached me in the same way that Tom Peters says the biomedical model approaches all humans, "as machines that operate within certain identifiable principles."[6]

Further compounding things is how the biomedical model influences doctors to interpret the sufferer's illness for them. Doctors do this by explaining the manifestations of illness as symptoms of the biological problem. In doing this, the doctor negatively defines how the sufferer experiences their illness and takes away from them their ability to find meaning in their experiences. Beverly Hall explains, "Because this model teaches that people can be diagnosed through the objective classification of their symptoms and scores on standardized tests, personal meaning, or what people, their families, and their cultures think is wrong with them, and the meanings that they attribute to their symptoms are not part of diagnostic considerations."[7]

Swinton uses schizophrenia as an example. He describes that the medical world writes off the patient's spiritual experiences that accompany the schizophrenia as pathological symptoms of the disease itself.[8] We could

---

5. Engel, "The Need for a New Medical Model," 40.
6. Peters, *Science, Theology and Ethics*, 285.
7. Hall, "The Psychiatric Model," 18.
8. Swinton, *Spirituality and Mental Health Care*, 146–47.

also apply Swinton's comments to depression. Depression is an inherently spiritual experience characterized by intense feelings of despair and apathy. According to the biomedical model, these feelings are pathological manifestations of the disease and have no inherent value. Indeed, their absence is desirable because it demonstrates a return to the patient's "normal" state. This happens because the biomedical model reduces everything to a biological root, and it assumes that it can control depression, and nearly all illnesses, through medical intervention alone.[9] Therefore, the biomedical model cannot help someone suffering from their disease to interpret and understand their suffering through their emotions.[10] For depression—a disease associated with loss of purpose and meaning—the biomedical model cannot offer someone who has lost these aspects of themselves any recourse other than the hope of fixing the biological dysfunction that caused the disease and its symptoms. The biomedical model cannot offer the depressed person any avenue to find meaning in their experiences. For the medical profession, the cause of depression is always biological.[11]

I called this chapter "Rescued but not Resuscitated" as a reference to Robert Taylor's death. The newspaper described how after his crewmates rescued him, their attempts to revive him by artificial resuscitation failed. That Robert was rescued but not resuscitated is a fitting analogy to what I experienced when medicine intervened in my life. In one way, the doctor's intervention rescued me, but the medical model in which he operated limited his response's effectiveness. The model failed him because it could not fully grasp the holistic nature of my depression. The medical model rescued me, but it did not have in its toolbox the means to resuscitate me. It helped me out, but it did not make me well.

THE BIOMEDICAL MODEL AS A FOLK THEORY

I did not know any of this information we are discussing when I saw my doctor for depression. It was not until years later, when I studied depression as part of my doctoral research, that I understood why my doctor approached things in the way he did. I do not mean to sound too critical of the biomedical model. I am very thankful for science's and medicine's involvement in our lives, because it has helped us immensely. Nor do I wish

---

9. Blazer, *The Age of Melancholy*, 8.
10. Swinton, "Healing Presence," 68.
11. Blazer, *The Age of Melancholy*, 4.

to sound critical of my doctor. He was a kind person and a competent doctor. He did his best and approached my treatment with respect. However, I realize now that his biomedical approach to my condition was as much caused by enculturation as it was by his medical training.

When we view the biomedical model as it operates within our western culture, it is evident that it forms the west's prominent cultural perspective about diseases. Therefore, it is the model to which we are naturally enculturated. This means that the biomedical model's understanding of diseases is the approach most of us will use to understand our illnesses. We will typically attribute the cause of any illness we experience to biological factors and exclude non-biological possibilities. This is true also of healthcare professionals who, like the rest of us, are enculturated to the biomedical model long before they begin their professional education.[12] Enculturation has a similar meaning to "socialization." Both are terms used to describe the lifelong process of learning our culture. None of us are born with a knowledge of our society and culture. It is something we learn as we grow and develop through generational transmission and as we navigate life. The things we learn as part of the process of enculturation act as a map for living life.

A model is a way of understanding and describing a belief system. Models do not exist by themselves. Instead, they are structures that help us explain natural phenomena and make sense of what is puzzling or disturbing. Because models must conform to a criterion relevant to culture, our culture's beliefs, explanations, and rules determine the phenomena in question, as well as the urgency with which we must resolve it. These views become our culturally created folk theories of health and disease. According to Helman, folk theories are models that we use to account for misfortune. He explains, since illness shares an identity with other kinds of adversity, and sufferers need explanations for their suffering, how a person describes their suffering will determine their folk theory. Their folk theory will then determine the way they act in the face of that misfortune. Therefore, folk theories have the power to shape the sufferer's understanding of the illness and the way they behave. Even if a patient has built their folk theory upon false premises, their folk theory still carries power and shapes their reality and their experience of the illness.[13] On the outside, the biomedical model stands in contrast to folk theories because it is a scientific model open to

---

12. Engel, "The Need for a New Medical Model," 40–41.
13. Helman, "Disease Versus Illness in General Practice," 549–50.

and designed to promote scientific inquiry. However, when we view the biomedical model as it operates within our western culture, we see that the biomedical model is not only a scientific model, it is also a cultural model that is acting in the same way as folk theories.[14] George Engel observes that the biomedical model has become a cultural imperative and has gained the status of dogma.[15]

When I remember my treatment, I realize now that my doctor acted consistently with the way culture conditioned him to act. He grew up in a western society that idolizes the biomedical model. He received his training in a medical school that further indoctrinated him, and he operated in a marketplace that believed in its preeminence. But not just him. I was also enculturated into this belief system. When my doctor told me I suffered from a mental health condition, I thought the preeminent healthcare model would save me. But, it did not save me because the biomedical model within which my doctor operated did not, and cannot, consider alternative sources to disease outside biological sources. The biomedical model can offer no recourse other than the hope of fixing the biological dysfunction that caused the disease through medical intervention, which was why my medication did not work. The biomedical model used medicine to fix the biological dysfunction, but it could not address the other contributors to my illness, such as personal, social, and spiritual sources. These had the biomedical model stumped. It had nothing in its arsenal to deal with the holistic nature of depression. To paraphrase Swinton, the holistic nature of depression means that therapy and drugs cannot necessarily solve or ease depression on their own.[16]

AN ALTERNATIVE TO THE BIOMEDICAL MODEL

In 2005, because of the biomedical model's limitations, Dan Blazer appealed to medicine to consider other theories of disease and dysfunction.[17] Blazer's appeal was nothing new because George Engel said the same back in 1977. Engel argued that incorporating a biopsychosocial model would cater to the growing unease among healthcare professionals that the biomedical model was not meeting health needs and that biomedical research did not

---

14. Engel, "The Need for a New Medical Model," 40.
15. Engel, "The Need for a New Medical Model," 40–41.
16. Swinton, *Spirituality and Mental Health Care*, 95–96.
17. Blazer, *The Age of Melancholy*, 21.

substantially affect research in human terms.[18] In response to these and other shortcomings, Engel suggested a biopsychosocial model of healthcare as an interdisciplinary model that takes the interconnection between biology, psychology, and socio-environmental factors seriously. Whereas, at best, the biomedical model only considered psychology and socio-environmental factors as stressors causing biological dysfunction, the biopsychosocial model understands psychological and socio-environmental factors as direct contributors to disease. Engel argued that a biopsychosocial model that considers all the factors associated with disease and illness would make it possible to understand why some patients experience illness in unique ways.[19] Daniel Sulmasy says that the biopsychosocial model of health and disease never caught on because the biomedical model has been so successful in treating diseases that the mainstream never had to consider an alternative.

Despite the biomedical model's success, Sulmasy criticizes it for viewing the patient as a detached object composed of a series of biochemical reactions that are open to investigation. The biomedical model reduces the person to a specimen consisting of systems, organs, and cells—a series of biochemical reactions. Sulmasy does not disregard the benefits of seeing people in this manner, nor how many people the biomedical model has helped. Nevertheless, he argues that a reductionist model is inadequate in serving the genuine need of patients, because it does not see the patient as a subject within a nexus of relationships. In response to the biomedical model and as an adaption of the biopsychosocial model, Sulmasy developed the biopsychosocial-spiritual model of health and disease based upon his understanding that healthcare professions should serve the patient's needs by viewing them as whole persons. He sees people as beings-in-relationship and illness as a disruption of these relationships. Spirituality plays a role because it describes an individual's or a community's relationship with the transcendent and their search for transcendent meaning.[20]

Sulmasy explains that throughout history, societies saw illness as a disruption in relationships. Most of these societies considered healing to be a religious activity through which people restored their relationships with each other and their god(s). In comparison, the scientific model sees disease as a breakdown of relationships within the body's biological functions,

---

18. Engel, "The Need for a New Medical Model," 49.
19. Engel, "The Need for a New Medical Model," 46
20. Sulmasy, "A Biopsychosocial-Spiritual Model," 25.

and healing comes (i.e., restoration of biological relationships) through medical intervention. However, Sulmasy asserts that the biomedical model is not holistic because the scientific view of disease operates within a closed system. Although it considers the disturbances in relationships inside the body, it does not consider disruptions in relationships that are outside the body (e.g., work and family life, preexisting coping patterns, and questions about one's relationship with the transcendent). Holistic healthcare, Sulmasy argues, must take into consideration all these things. He writes, "What genuinely holistic health care means then is a system of health care that attends to all of the disturbed relationships of the ill person as a whole, restoring those that can be restored, even if the person is not thereby completely restored to perfect wholeness."[21] Because he defines spirituality as the means through which a person relates to the transcendent, he proposes that genuine holistic healthcare must also address the totality of the patient's relational existence, i.e., physical, psychological, social, and spiritual. Although the biopsychosocial model placed the patient within a nexus that included their mental state and their surrounding interpersonal relationships, it did not consider patient spirituality and death.[22]

I appeal to Sulmasy's research because I now see the biomedical model's inability to view humans as beings that operate within the nexus of relationships as a stumbling block towards a holistic approach to healing and helping people live fuller lives when confronted with suffering. For myself, there were areas in my life that caused my depression for which a biological understanding could not account. This meant that I would not receive healing from depression until these areas of my life received healing first. We will discuss this in another chapter, but I will say that it was not until I experienced the holistic biblical concepts of *sozo* and *shalom* through Christ's redeeming grace that my depression was cured. These are concepts which the biomedical model cannot account for, but the biopsychosocial-spiritual model can because it recognizes the spiritual dynamic in our lives and focuses on holism. Therefore, this model acts as a preferred model that establishes the foundation for this book. The biomedical model's empiricist foundation does not allow this underpinning.

---

21. Sulmasy, "A Biopsychosocial-Spiritual Model," 25–26.
22. Sulmasy, "A Biopsychosocial-Spiritual Model," 24.

5

What is Health?

OUR CULTURE'S VIEW OF HEALTH

THROUGHOUT THIS BOOK, WE have touched on definitions of health, but we have never defined it. This chapter attempts a description by comparing our culture's view of health with the biblical view of health. One intriguing definition—and I do not think the authors from whom I quote meant it as such—is this: "Health is that thing we long for only when we do not have it."[1] This statement explains that health, in some ways, is something we know we have or do not have. It is something we do not miss or think about until we recognize its absence. In this regard, health has subjective and personal qualities to it. However, because we live and grow in a society and culture with distinct views of health and illness, our "personal" understanding of health is not unique to us. We received it over hundreds of years of cultural development through our parents, families, friends, school, the things we read, the pictures we look at, and media. Therefore, our society and culture play a vital role in constructing how we understand and experience health, thereby shaping our beliefs, how we act, and those things that give our lives meaning and purpose.

Dirk Jakobus Louw says that health has become a cultural value in western culture and is the "epitome of human striving."[2] He describes how our culture is obsessed with health and takes health beyond relief from

---

1. Shuman and Meador, *Heal Thyself*, 12.
2. Louw, "Space and Place in the Healing of Life," 428.

sickness and views it as optimum performance and efficiency in every part of life.³ Consumerism provides a vehicle for this view of health, driving our needs and desires while making us think we can fulfill them by consuming goods and services. As Joel James Shuman and Keith G. Meador say, "The market promises us the things we want, including happiness and health and freedom from suffering and anguish, and just to the extent we participate in its enticement, it continues to form us to expect even more of the same."⁴

Consumerism influences our wish for physical and emotional health. We see things such as faith, religion, medicine, lifestyle, and relationships as commodities that we can buy to fulfill our desires and to ease our suffering as quickly as possible.⁵ Our society's commodification of such things links to our belief that we can "make healthy" those areas of our lives that are "unhealthy." An enormous part of this relates to how we build our image of health around our self-interests.⁶ This means we consider ourselves healthy so long as our lives fit within our societal and personal criteria of health. For instance, someone may think his life is healthy so long as his body is fit, he looks handsome, he drives an expensive car, and he has an excellent job. Yet, he does not consider those areas of his life unhealthy where he has a bad attitude, has broken relationships, and is mishandling his finances. Individualism's union with consumerism enables him to pick and choose those areas of life that he wants to develop and make healthy, against those areas of his life he is happy to neglect.

Society often speaks of emotional health, economic health, financial health, relationship health, as well as other types of "health." What is notable is that society teaches us we can find healing and health in these areas of life if we only spend money on them. We can buy a self-help book to help us develop emotional health, or we can spend money and enroll in a financial help class to help us get out of debt. We can pay for yoga classes, pay for a counselor's services to help with our relationships, or join Weight Watchers to help us lose weight and regain our health. There is nothing wrong with these, but a hidden impetus exists behind these acts that reveal we believe we can invest in those areas of health we consider more important, and we can pay to be healthier. But by paying, we dilute some of our own

---

3. Louw, "Space and Place in the Healing of Life," 428, citing S. J. Hunt, *Alternative Religions. A Sociological Introduction* (Hampshire: Ashgate, 2003), 183–84.
4. Shuman and Meador, *Heal Thyself*, 11.
5. Shuman and Meador, *Heal Thyself*, 11; Blazer, *The Age of Melancholy*, 10.
6. Shuman and Meador, *Heal Thyself*, 10.

responsibility to be healthy, because we place the burden on the product we bought. If it does not work to our expectations, then we assume the product was faulty. I remember hearing a dietician comment, "Any diet works if you stick to it. The trouble is that few people will stick to it." So, again, the idea exists that we can pick and choose health and reach our goals through the products the market offers. As Swinton notes, health is a commodity that one can sell or buy in today's western consumer society[7]—a commodity which, if we follow our spending habits as individuals and as a society, will reveal those aspects of health that we find most valuable.

As the next chapter will show, western culture medicalized disease and ill health throughout the last century. When considered alongside our culture's emphasis on consumerism, the commodification of health through pharmaceuticals emerged as the obvious way to restore health. As a result, we now place a very high expectation on medicine's role in our lives. As this relates to depression, our society medicalized depression by believing that the cause of depression is always solely biological.[8] Because of this, our medical culture describes depression's manifestations away as simply being symptoms,[9] which robs the patient from finding meaning and wholeness in the broader context of the illness through any medium other than prescription drugs. However, many of us accept this medicalized approach because our western culture is "therapeutic" and has conditioned us to satisfy our needs and desires without correctly ordering them.[10] Culture drives us to satiate our suffering by the quickest means possible. Under such circumstances, we naturally turn to medicine for help, which, as Rudy Nydegger says, is "overused and misused by many who are looking for a quick and easy solution to a very complex disorder."[11]

Shuman and Meador say that our culture has a very implicit belief that one day medicine and technology will extinguish sickness and all other limitations from our lives.[12] They quote Daniel Callahan, who says, "Hardly anyone speaks openly of immortality as the aim [of medicine], but that is beside the point; it is built into the research imperative."[13] However, find-

---

7. Swinton, "Understanding Health."
8. Blazer, *The Age of Melancholy*, 10.
9. Swinton, *Spirituality and Mental Health Care*, 156–57.
10. Shuman and Meador, *Heal Thyself*, 80.
11. Nydegger, *Understanding and Treating Depression*, 42.
12. Shuman and Meador, *Heal Thyself*, 9–10.
13. Shuman and Meador, *Heal Thyself*, 10, citing Daniel Callahan, "Death and the

ing healing in pharmaceuticals is a long-shot, because the medical model assumes that an individual's biological vulnerability to depression is innate, making prevention impossible.[14] Therefore, for depression, and any other disease, using medication is more about disease management and control than about cure. Because prevention is impossible, questions that determine the treatment's effectiveness drive medical research instead of disease prevention being the driving factor.[15] If this surprises us, it is because, in the "general milieu of economic expansion and technological optimism, we are schooled to expect that the market and the laboratory, between them, will fulfill all of our problems."[16]

The commodified role that medicine plays in managing and controlling depression's innateness takes an interesting turn when we consider it alongside how western culture elevates our mind's function. Our culture is hyper-cognitive in the way that we place a great emphasis on the role of our brain.[17] This idea developed with the work of René Descartes (1596–1650). He separated the body from the mind by asserting the body's autonomy to the mind. As his ideas developed, he concluded that the mind could live without the body. At first, he maintained causality so that one could affect the other. However, as his understanding developed, Descartes believed that the mind could live without the body, and that the mind contained the "total essence" of the human being. He rationalized that the only part of his humanity of which he could be sure was his thinking.[18] Other thinkers came along and developed Descartes' view, so that over time, mind and body dualism emerged. This affected the contemporary understanding of humanity by linking being human with cognitive functioning. A value-based system for being a person developed, and our society came to value cognition above other human capacities.[19]

Within today's hyper-cognitive environment, depression and other diseases of the mind are problematic because they raise critical questions concerning what it means to be human. When people lose their minds in today's culture, they literally lose a central part of their personhood. They

---

Research Imperative," *The New England Journal of Medicine*, 342 (2000) 654.
14. Blazer, *The Age of Melancholy*, 10.
15. Blazer, *The Age of Melancholy*, 11.
16. Shuman and Meador, *Heal Thyself*, 10.
17. Dewing, "Personhood and Dementia," 5.
18. Brown, "Aquinas' Alternative to Cartesian Dualism," 2.
19. Dewing, "Personhood and Dementia," 5.

lose the thing that makes them human. Problems emerge when we link our hyper-cognitive outlook to personhood with our commodified approach to medicine as a tool to manage and control depression. Not least, medicine becomes the means through which we turn patients who are losing their personhood (i.e., those with mental health problems) back into persons. However, because our medical model views disease as innate, the notion then exists that those who have depression, or any disease, were biologically destined to develop it, and thereby lose their personhood in some capacity.

THE BIBLICAL VIEW OF HEALTH

Western society sees health as the absence of disease or abnormalities. We interpret health and approach it within the context of our western consumer society so that it becomes a commodified personal and social norm. Seeing health as a commodity reveals that western culture has a relatively shallow understanding of health compared to the Old Testament. Wilkinson describes how the Old Testament authors were not as interested in their bodies' anatomy and physiology as we are. They referred to their anatomical parts, but they linked these parts with issues of morality and spirituality. Those in the Old Testament approached life by focusing on the quality of life rather than the quantity of life. One way they expressed this quality was through the Hebrew word *shalom*. *Shalom* encapsulates concepts such as righteousness, obedience, strength, fertility, and longevity. We would better understand *shalom* by using our contemporary understanding of the word "wellbeing" to describe it.[20] Even then, the Old Testament understanding of *shalom* is even broader and more holistic than our definition of wellbeing, and it includes such concepts as the wholeness of being and the uprightness of character within the context of holiness.[21] "Wholeness" and "holiness" are terms used to express the state of a person's relationship with God. Both words imply a standard, i.e., God's perfect character.[22] Therefore, true *shalom* or wellbeing comes from God, because only through him do we find true wholeness and fulfillment. Thus, the Old Testament developed its idea of health around a person's response to God and obedience to his will.

We cannot become holy by our efforts, nor can we develop our wellbeing by ourselves. God must aid us. Considering that modern society views

---

20. Wilkinson, *The Bible and Healing*, 11–13.
21. Wilkinson, *The Bible and Healing*, 17.
22. Wilkinson, *The Bible and Healing*, 18.

health as an individualistic value that we must strive toward, the suggestion that we need God's help to grow in health and wellbeing might surprise us. Nevertheless, authentic wellbeing and health only exist in the love and will of God. *Shalom* is "experienced in a right relationship to God; it is experienced communally; it is experienced in an exceptional way within the family system and should be expanded to the whole of creation. *Shalom*, therefore, denotes the fullness of life."[23] In the Old Testament, health includes wholeness and the rightness of our relationships,[24] and our correct behavior within those relationships.[25] God sets the requirements for what is acceptable and not acceptable in these relationships. Therefore, when we live our lives according to God's relationship requirements, we experience *shalom* (i.e., health and wellbeing). However, if our lifestyle is inconsistent with God's requirements, then it leads to ill-health. Thus, normative *shalom* behavior leads to *shalom* (i.e., health), and non-normative *shalom* behavior leads to non-*shalom* (i.e., ill-health).

If we are to be less tactful, we could refer to non-normative *shalom* behavior as sin. Jay Sklar defines sin as "anything contrary to God and his purpose for this world." This is problematic because, as Sklar explains, God's purpose for this world is that it might reflect his character and be in relationship with Him. Sin ruins this purpose because it acts as "relational poison" that leads sinners down the path of self-destruction and destroys their relationship within themselves, with others, with creation, and with God.[26] That sin destroys relationship structures is problematic when we consider the fact that the biblical idea of health is very much relational. Fortunately, the redemptive work of Jesus Christ is God's answer to sin. Through Jesus' death and resurrection, God showed his love towards humanity (Rom 5:8) and his desire to expel sin (Matt 9:2–8). Therefore, the New Testament builds its understanding of health upon the Old Testament view of *shalom* and further asserts that we can only find health and wholeness as we live in relationship with God. As in the Old Testament, the New Testament grounds health in God's life and perfection, so only through fellowship and obedience to him can humans enjoy and share in authentic

---

23. Louw, "Space and Place in the Healing of Life," 430.
24. Wilkinson, *The Bible and Healing*, 12.
25. Wilkinson, *The Bible and Healing*, 20.
26. Sklar, "Sin."

health, life, and perfection.²⁷ Obedience to God comes by sharing in his life and holiness through Jesus. Wilkinson says,

> Nothing could be healthier than the life of God producing in human beings that wholeness, soundness and righteousness which constitute true health and holiness. This relationship of divine and human life is a vital and basic element in the New Testament concept of health. Life apart from God is mere existence and duration. Health forms no necessary part of it and people who live apart from God may therefore lack health all the days of their life. But where human life is infused with the life of God and lived in a close and constant relationship with him, there is life indeed. Here life means health and health is life itself.²⁸

The New Testament provides us with a complete understanding of health by interpreting it through Jesus' revelation. In this respect, *shalom* is a person. The Hebrews believed that the Messiah would be the Prince of *Shalom* (Isa 9:6; Zech 9:10). Through the incarnation, Jesus grounds *shalom* in his person. To paraphrase Swinton, Jesus is the bearer of *shalom* who gives his peace—his *shalom*—to those who follow him: "Peace I leave with you, My peace I give to you; not as the world gives do I give to you" (John 14:27). Swinton summarizes, "True health—shalom—is not something that can be understood outside of Jesus."²⁹

Looking at how our western culture understands health compared to how the Bible understands health helps explain why the antidepressants that my doctor prescribed did not heal me of depression. They did not cure me because they were created on the assumption that my biological vulnerability to depression was innate, so the antidepressants focused on managing and controlling my depression, rather than on curing. I explained how the antidepressants were like putting a fresh coat of paint over rotten wood in an earlier chapter. They only covered up what was lacking or wrong on the inside of me. Looking back now, I can relate to what Jesus said to the Pharisees when he referred to them as whitewashed tombs: "For you are like whitewashed tombs which indeed appear beautiful outwardly, but inside are full of dead men's bones and all uncleanness" (Matt 23:27). Jesus spoke to religious hypocrites, but his criticism applies to how I remember my prescription's effectiveness. The pills acted as a veneer that covered up

---

27. Wilkinson, *The Bible and Healing*, 26.
28. Wilkinson, *The Bible and Healing*, 29.
29. Swinton, "From Health to Shalom," 235.

something unclean inside me. And every time I returned to the doctor for my check-ups, he whitewashed the uncleanness by increasing the dosage.

Swinton describes depression as a spiritual experience that relates to the whole person. Its holistic nature means that therapy and drugs alone cannot necessarily solve or ease it. Instead, depression requires a holistic response.[30] Swinton's observation concurs with my experience. My doctor's prescription did not heal my depression, because it could not fix the problem's root cause. A biochemical imbalance in my brain may have caused my depression, which the antidepressants sought to control, but the antidepressants could not control what caused the biochemical imbalance. What caused the biochemical imbalance was more in line with the biblical understanding of health, and only by experiencing *shalom* through Jesus Christ, could I be healed from depression.

MY ENTRANCE INTO BIBLICAL HEALTH: HOW GOD CURED ME OF DEPRESSION

About two years after trying to commit suicide at the beach, I went with my mother and my young nephew to a town 30 miles away for a summer vacation where our family had a second home. Maria, another of my cousins, lived there with her mom and sister. Her dad, my mom's brother, had passed away many years before. Maria's family were Christians, and they attended a church called Zion Tabernacle on Hope Street.

At the same time when I was there, a guest speaker visited the church from America, and Maria invited me to go to one of the evening services. Although I did not want to go, the promise of free food afterward compelled me. Having attended a funeral at that church a few years before, I knew that the food the church catered was usually delicious. However, as delicious as the food would be, it was nowhere near tasty enough to warrant having to listen to discordant Christian music and to hear a preacher drone on for two hours. I, therefore, timed my arrival at church to coincide with the end of the service. I crept in the main doors, avoided the few ushers, and headed straight to the kitchen and reception area where they served the food.

A teenage girl who helped prepare the food approached me as I waited for the overdue service to end and for my cousin to come in with the other bored and hungry attendees. This girl knew my cousin and had heard that

---

30. Swinton, *Spirituality and Mental Health Care*, 95–96.

I was visiting, so we began chatting. At first, we talked about the weather and things like that, but soon her Christian-radar perked up and she detected that I was not "one of them." I was one of those pitiful sinners whom her pastor droned on about, week in and week out, who needed saving. I was free-game who needed to hear about God. At the least she could tell her Bible study group how she tried to evangelize me the next time she attended. They would give her a feather in her cap for sure.

She rattled on explaining how (and I paraphrase) "God sent his Son to earth to free humanity from the clutches of evil so that we can live with God in this life and into the next. But we must accept his act of liberation. We have to apologize to him for the way we've lived our lives and accept him as our savior."

I remember thinking, "How dare you tell me about a God, who probably doesn't exist, and suggest I must apologize to him for the way I've lived my life! It should be the other way around. If God exists, then he should apologize to me for how my life is!"

I only had to listen to her droning on about Jesus for a few moments more, because the attendees began piling through the door, seeking their tea and home-bakes. With her attention diverted, I escaped. No longer did I have to listen to her nonsense.

Although there was no alcohol, I got on with my cousin and her friends. My nephew was there too, so we hung out until it got late, and then my nephew and I went back home. My nephew went upstairs to bed while I went out to the back yard, via the kitchen, to have a quick smoke. The time alone recharged me, and the cool summer breeze provided some solace, allowing me to think. I enjoyed reflecting, and this was the first time that things were quiet since the teenage girl spoke to me in church. But rather than thinking about other things, I kept on thinking about what she said, which probably had something to do with the arrogance with which she spoke. I mean, who was she to say I needed God and had to apologize to him? God did not exist, and if he did, then why should I apologize to him? I assume he had better things to do than wait around for my apology.

I had heard others speak about Jesus before. What the girl said did not differ much from those people, but there was something different about how she said it. There was something about her that told me she believed this God stuff. She looked happy enough too. I could not imagine that she spent her nights drinking and thinking of ways to kill herself. Then the question struck my mind: "Could she have met God?" She spoke as if she had met him.

I shrugged off the idea. "No, that was impossible. God did not exist."

But what if he did?

I took the last puff of my cigarette and threw it on the ground. Either way, if he did or did not exist, I was going to find out. I had nothing to live for anyway, so what was the harm in looking for him? Self-harm and suicide had not worked for me. I was a coward, or else I would have topped myself long ago. The least I could do was find out if God existed.

Tip-toeing back into the kitchen, I checked to see if everyone was in their beds. It was about 1 or 2 am, so everybody was—but I just wanted to make sure. I did not want anyone to come into the kitchen for a midnight snack and catch me trying to find God.

It was the weirdest thing in the world to do, but since no one was watching, I kneeled in the middle of the kitchen's wooden floor. I waited for a bit and got the impression I needed to break the silence. Eventually, I mumbled, "God, if you're real, then I want to meet you, and if you're real, then I want to know you the same way the girl at the church seems to."

Silence.

The silence strengthened my resolve. Determination flooded through me, and I set my knees against the hard floor. I would stay on my knees until God responded and proved his existence, or until the silence revealed that he did not exist. Either way, tonight I would know for sure if God was real. Tomorrow, I would have no doubts.

More silence.

Time ticked by for as long as it took for my knees to go numb. Then some more time passed. It was hard to track the time, but hours passed—and with each passing hour, my resolve increased. Time acted as a mortar. I had asked God to show himself, and I would kneel for as long as necessary.

More silence.

"Robert," a voice said, "if you stick with me, then I'll stick with you."

The words came from deep inside me and all around me. They penetrated something deep in my soul, and a bulwark inside me that I was unaware of came crumbling down. A torrent of revelation surged through me, and in an instant, I saw God. As if from nowhere, I saw God's glory in my inner being. The enormity of his righteousness, mercy, and his character over-awed me.

I knew that I was sobbing. Tears streaked my face, but they did not flow from a stream of self-pity at my own hopelessness. They poured from the realization that up to that point, I had lived my life in total defiance to a good God who wanted what was best for me. I beheld his holiness, and I saw the repulsiveness of my sin and my lifestyle. Under the weight of conviction, I heard myself say, "Sorry." But I probably said much more.

Who knows how long I knelt, but eventually, I wiped the tears from my face and scrambled to my numb feet to search the house for a Bible. With my legs and feet unwieldy from the hours of kneeling, I quickly searched the nearby rooms until I found an old sun-faded picture study Bible. Thumbing the mammoth book open, I read the first thing I saw.

> "I am the true vine, and My Father is the vinedresser. Every branch in Me that does not bear fruit He takes away; and every branch that bears fruit He prunes, that it may bear more fruit. You are already clean because of the word which I have spoken to you. Abide in Me, and I in you. As the branch cannot bear fruit of itself, unless it abides in the vine, neither can you, unless you abide in Me.
>
> I am the vine, you are the branches. He who abides in Me, and I in him, bears much fruit; for without Me you can do nothing. If anyone does not abide in Me, he is cast out as a branch and is withered; and they gather them and throw them into the fire, and they are burned. If you abide in Me, and My words abide in you, you will ask what you desire, and it shall be done for you. By this My Father is glorified, that you bear much fruit; so you will be My disciples."
>
> (John 15:1–8)

My heart thumped and my mind heaved as something inside me clicked into place. The power of what I read raced through me and jolted me. Everything became clear. In an instant, I understood God's role, what just happened to me, and my place in the grand scheme of things. Peace and joy surged through me, and thankfulness filled my mouth.

When I got on my knees a few hours before, I was a hell-deserving man who was experiencing hell in his life—and now I stood up with my heart renewed in God's sight. The next morning when I awoke, everything looked different. The grass looked greener, and the sky shone brighter. I felt free and liberated. I knew I had met God the night before and that my life had a purpose. At once, I stopped smoking and drinking, because the need was no longer there. The depression vanished, and my mindset changed entirely. I stopped taking the antidepressants straight away.

When I returned to Aberdeen from my vacation, I had my scheduled check-up with the doctor. I told him I had met God through Jesus Christ, that he had healed me of depression, and that I had stopped taking the medication.

My doctor had no substantial response. To his due, he did not coax me into taking the medication again just to make sure. All he said was, "You certainly look happier." I never saw him after that.

I knew when I returned to Aberdeen I would face challenges. My old life was there, including my friends, drinking buddies, and reputation. Plus, I had no Christian friends, knew nothing about churches to know which one to attend. I did not know what to do, but God had given me something precious, and I would not jeopardize it. There is a passage in the Bible of a man who found a pearl of great value and sold everything that he had to buy it (Matt 13:45–46). That's how I viewed my salvation. It was so precious to me that I gave up everything to have it. I cut off every tie with my old friends. I told them I met Jesus—and I left it there. If they called and asked me to go out, I refused. After a while, they stopped calling. The salvation that God gave me was so precious that I determined to do anything to keep it. I sat in my apartment alone for the first few months that I was a Christian because I did not have any Christian friends, and it took me a while to build relationships at the church I began attending. However, despite the loneliness, I resolved not to put myself in a situation of compromise.

CHAPTER SUMMARY

I am glad for the biomedical model, and I believe God works through medicine. I have seen it work in my life and in my family's lives, especially when the children were teething or ill at 4 am—ibuprofen and acetaminophen worked wonders. However, there were parts of my life that medicine could not reach and fix. And the reason why medicine could not reach and repair these areas was because medicine could not make my relationship right with God. There is no pill for salvation. Only being introduced to and accepting Jesus as my Savior could heal and deliver me from depression. In Jesus, I experienced *shalom*, which refers to "to a positive state of complete fulfillment and a sense of destiny as it emanates from God and his will for a humane life in dignity and righteousness."[31] Because health includes harmony in relationships, then true fulfillment, or *shalom*, comes by being in a

---

31. Louw, "Space and Place in the Healing of Life," 429.

correct relationship with the person through whom God revealed himself. Amos Yong says, "Christian salvation is never an abstract transaction but is a palpably experiential and personal, with wider effects. When lives are touched redemptively by God, things are changed, behaviors are redirected, and salvific transformation unleashed."[32] As such, salvation "moves one out of compulsive, addictive, obsessive patterns of behavior toward more healthy relationships with oneself, other persons, and God."[33]

---

32. Yong, *Renewing Christian Theology*, 252.
33. Peck, "What is Christian Spirituality?," 1.

6

Depression Returns

THE YEARS PASS AND DEPRESSION RETURNS

AFTER I GOT SAVED and the summer vacation ended, I returned to my undergraduate studies at the University of Aberdeen. Being a little bit of an introvert now that I was no longer drinking and being unsure of church life, it naturally took me a few months before I began attending a vibrant local church, which turned out to be Pentecostal. My salvation experience filled me with a sense of purpose. All the hopelessness and despair disappeared, and my mental health changed overnight. I felt a deep sense of calling, and I dedicated my life to God's service to share what he had done for me. With this new lease on life, I threw myself into my local church with all that was in me. I attended every service, and I was involved heavily in the church community and ministry, especially the university student ministry. The ministry leader was a man named Frank, who, with his wife and family, had dedicated their lives to student ministry. He was a pleasant, kind man, about 25 years my senior, whom I deeply respected. As he did with every student in the group, we regularly met for coffee and chatted. During this early phase of my Christian life, I was introduced to just how much coffee Christians drink.

I served in the student ministry for about nine months and was close to graduating when Frank and I met at a coffee shop one sunny afternoon in March. I felt close enough to him to share my testimony and to tell him that my newfound purpose was taking me down the path of service and ministry, so I intended to pursue theological education after graduation.

I remember the way that Frank looked at me when I told him my salvation testimony, which was a condensed version from the last chapter. He stared at me. His brown eyes were expressionless, and his graying goatee hid any sign of emotion that his lips might have revealed.

"And ever since then," I continued to explain, "I've got a purpose and a reason for living. I feel called to ministry. I want to live for others the way you do and see them reach their full potential in Christ."

Frank sat back with his arms folded. A passing waitress had to squeeze behind him. Her polite smile revealed annoyance. "Look, Robert. I don't think God's called you."

What? I must have heard him wrong. Surely, he would not say that! I looked around the coffee shop for an object to focus on as my mind searched for something to say. The waitress took a long way around from the table that she served instead of passing behind Frank's chair.

"If I was you," said Frank leaning back in his chair as if to keep his distance, "I'd continue to do what you're doing. Get a job, live normally, and get on with life."

"You don't think I should go to seminary or continue in ministry education?"

He shook his head.

"What of the spiritual things I'm experiencing and the way God's moving in my life? I think God's telling me I'm called and that I should further educate myself."

"I was like you once. Many people are. They get saved and are full of excitement for God. Over time, it'll go away. The spiritual high you're experiencing now will go away as you mature and grow up in Christ."

My mouth dried. Wasn't he supposed to be encouraging me instead of dashing the newfound purpose that shaped my life against the rocks? If I had no purpose, then what was the point of being a Christian?

He glanced at his watch. "I need to go." Frank took his brown leather organizer from the table and put it in his laptop bag.

With the efficiency with which he organized his day, he had just organized the rest of my life. I promised myself there and then that I would never be the same as Frank and the others whom he spoke of, whose experience of God disappeared as they became more mature in Christ.

That was my first disappointment as a Christian, and I found it challenging. I had walked with Christ and attended church for less than a year, so when Frank told me I was not ministry material, it caused much upset and crushed the purpose that shaped my life. In many ways, that meeting foreshadowed what I later observed as a common phenomenon among many church members whom I met in the UK and the USA: the feeling that God had called them, yet they remained on the outside looking into church life confused as to what role God has called them to play.

I wondered if everything that I thought God spoke to me about my purpose and calling were true. I thought, "Why be a Christian if I have no purpose?" However, through a time of soul-searching and prayer, I became convinced that my deep sense of purpose came from God, so I chose not to listen to Frank.

After graduating with my undergraduate degree, I moved 100 miles back to Pittenweem and began attending a church in Methil, about 15 miles away from my hometown. There, I continued with my Christian life and served in any part of the church where I could. One day the opportunity arose to go to seminary in the USA, so I went there as a student to study. I studied hard at the seminary and took part in whatever ministry opportunity I found, whether it was walking the streets of downtown Tulsa distributing food and evangelizing the homeless, serving undergraduate students as a Teaching Assistant, or being part of my local church's prayer team.

I met my wife in America. We shared the same love for God and feeling of purpose. After a time of intense prayer and fasting, we felt that it was the Lord's will for us to be together, so we married. When we graduated, we returned to the UK to the same city where I lived when I was a member of the student ministry. Four years had passed, and God had called Frank home during the time I had been away. I began studying for a Ph.D., which we foresaw as the Lord's next step, and we got plugged into the same vibrant Pentecostal church of which I was a member before when I served in the student ministry under Frank. The church welcomed us with open arms. We took part in church life, and we served with joyful and thankful hearts. However, after a year or so, I realized that our abilities, gifts, time, and presence were never enough.

I write this with the utmost respect because I have some fond memories, and I am grateful to have been part of such a great local church. I admire the pastoral staff and leadership team, and I still have friends at that church. For me, though, the church system seemed to want more and more. Church program after church program reinforced this adage: God's grace may have saved you, but the church will judge you by your level of service. The words of Jack Hawkins' Quintus Arrius to Charlton Heston's

Ben-Hur echoed around me, "We keep you alive to serve this ship. So row well and live."

When I spent time alone in my private devotions, Jesus affirmed me. I felt loved and accepted. The Spirit told me I had a purpose and a role in God's Kingdom, but I experienced the opposite when I attended church and took part in church life. To God, I was a somebody who meant something, but I felt like a number to the church. This confused me, because I saw the local church as the demonstration of Jesus' body on earth. Therefore, Jesus was giving me two different messages. In the prayer closet, he told me he loved me and had called me for a purpose, but he demonstrated to me through his church Body that I was a cog in the system with no inherent value other than to take part.

As a Pentecostal, my experience of God affirmed my revelation of God, which developed my knowledge of God. Wolfgang Vondey explains that Pentecostals interpret their life experiences through a Spirit-led reading of the Scripture and community interaction (e.g., sermons, prayer meetings, Bible studies, online media, etc.). This contributes towards their everyday encounters with Christ and facilitates their Christian formation and growth.[1] Through daily interactions with the Spirit in their lives, Pentecostals expect to experience God, and by experiencing him, they interpret their reality and find their identity. However, because my revelation of God in my prayer closet did not complement what I experienced in my local church, I experienced dissonance that caused me to question my Christian reality and identity. Quite simply, things were not adding up.

In Romans 10:11, Paul says, "Whoever believes on Him will not be put to shame." This scripture was one of those by which I lived my life, but my experience left me feeling as if the Lord had shamed me for believing that I had a purpose and calling. I abandoned the notion of doing a Ph.D., and I completed university prematurely by graduating with a Postgraduate Diploma. I went through several temporary jobs until, after much discouragement, the Lord blessed me with a job in the Oil and Gas industry with excellent career potential. While my career flourished, I continued to attend church and I never missed a service. I exhausted myself doing everything that the church system required of me, and I never dreamed of being called by God again. Discouraged, I did what Frank had told me to do: I got a job, lived normally, and got on with life.

---

1. Vondey, *Pentecostal Theology*, 15.

I am not surprised that under such circumstances, depression returned over the weeks and months. It was never as bad as it was during those years before when I did not know Jesus. I never tried to commit suicide or to self-harm again, but the thoughts were there and were gaining ground in my life. And with each inch the depression gained, I seemed to enter more deeply into a vicious cycle of negative thought patterns that grew harder to fight. Swinton says, "If a person can no longer relate to God, and if their self-image and interpretation of the world is dependent on their experience of God, then to experience such abandonment is, in a very real sense, to lose part of themselves."[2] I experienced that abandonment and loss of identity and self, which further blocked my ability to engage with and interpret any formational God-experiences I continued to have inside or outside the church. My outlook was pessimistic and apathetic as my life became stale and pointless. Abandonment and despair filled my life. Frank's words echoed in my mind: "I don't think you're called."

IDENTITY AND PURPOSE

Looking back now, I realize I was so focused on my identity and calling that when I was faced with the conflicting messages I received in my devotions and my church, these created the perfect breeding ground for depression. The years that I spent on both sides of the Atlantic, consuming contemporary Christianity's glossy multimedia rhetoric-barrage of identity and purpose, formed me into a perfect candidate for this type of dissonance.

Identity and purpose are things that our culture, inside and outside Christianity, focuses on a lot nowadays. Media of all sorts bombard us, saying we have an identity and a purpose, and that we sell ourselves short if we do not direct these into a goal or calling. There is a lot of pressure for us to have a vision and to change our world by fulfilling our God-given purpose. No college or church whiteboard is safe from the scribbles of well-meaning teachers and coaches, all over the country, telling us that if we discover our identity in Christ, then we will find our purpose. Then, once we know our purpose, we can walk in our calling. For example, a college student still has to declare her major and does not know what career path to take. She attends a church service where the speaker takes the audience through a step-by-step process of finding their identity in Christ, from which they discern their purpose, which leads them to know what God has called them

---

2. Swinton, *Spirituality and Mental Health*, 115.

to do with their lives. The college student goes back to her dorm and begins an intensive period of Bible study and self-reflection in order to find out who she is in Christ. During this period, she realizes that God has given her an aptitude for teaching, and she figures God has called her to be a teacher, so she declares her major as education. Another example is: A homemaker's last child flies the nest. After being a homemaker for twenty-five years, her identity collapses because her purpose and calling up to this point has been to raise her four children. She no longer knows who she is or why she is here. Her life promises nothing but emptiness. Unsure of her new season in life, she goes to the same service as the student and hears the same message. She goes home, dedicates some time to reestablishing her identity, and the Lord encourages her. She starts posting the encouragement that she receives in her private devotions on social media, and before long, she realizes God has gifted her in this area. She discerns that God has given her a new purpose in life and called her to encourage other empty-nesters. These two examples do nothing to detail the complexities involved in this process of moving from identity, to purpose, to calling. And although I thank the Lord for those for whom this strategy works, I am probably one of the few Christians who found this approach more harmful than good.

My life has never been a linear progression from points A to B to C. My life is more of a squiggle that, over time, heads in the right direction. Although the church's analytical preaching of identity, purpose, and calling has done more to trip me up than to help me, I have come to terms with this rhetoric over the years, and I do not take it as seriously as I once did. I now focus more on God's promises for my life and less on his purpose and my calling. As the hymn *Amazing Grace* says, "The Lord has promised good to me." I give these words preeminence over what is scribbled on the whiteboard.

Nevertheless, as I considered my second bout of depression alongside the church's linear approach of preaching the progression from identity to purpose to calling, it is evident that these are, themselves, attributes that depression destroys. Depression attacks these attributes by eroding the foundational aspect of a person's being that constructs and interprets their reality. This is the place where Christian identity is formed. Depression attacks the nexus of human experience, where the Christian meets God through the Spirit. Therefore, depression sufferers experience abandonment and loss of identity, which further blocks their ability to engage with and interpret formational God-experiences. When Christians suffer from depression, they are unable to progress from identity to purpose to calling. Depression has them at a standstill, isolating them from their God-given identity, purpose, and calling.

A common question that might arise is this: "Since depression attacks this nexus through which we experience God and interpret our reality, then why not approach our identity and purpose through a more cognitive approach? Instead of focusing on our experiences, why not focus on what the Bible says about who we are in Jesus?" This is a logical question that goes hand-in-hand with the general observation that crusades and youth events elicit a great deal of emotions for the things of God. Attendees are "on fire for Christ." However, after a few weeks, the emotions run out, and believers are as spiritually dry and lukewarm as they were before the event. The logical solution, then, is to establish and ground their emotions in the Word. "You don't have to feel like you're saved as long as you know that you're saved." Or, "You don't have to feel like God loves you, as long as you know that God loves you." This is pretty much how Frank approached me. He tried to bring my newfound spiritual experiences (i.e., the emotions that I felt) of being saved down to earth. For me, though, his approach did more harm than good.

The suggestion to balance the experience of God with knowledge of God in order to stop depression from cutting off the experiential aspect of the Christian life, although admirable, displays a flawed understanding of what Christian experience is. When we speak about the Christian experience, we are talking about more than a feeling or an emotion. We are talking about the place where the gospel is "grounded, embodied, interpreted, and lived out" through the locus of the Spirit.[3] For Keener, experience means believing the Bible to the point that our belief leads to faith in action.[4] So, when we speak of depression negatively affecting our ability to experience God and, therefore, hindering our ability to construct and interpret reality, we are talking about more than an emotional disruption that we can tackle by a simple cognitive response of reading the Bible, confessing the Word, and listening to more sermons on the internet. The kind of experience that we are on about here is a holistic understanding that considers every aspect of what it means to be human. And based on this understanding of experience, depression is equally as holistic and affects every area of the sufferer's life. Depression is a very tangible and down-to-earth experience that works

---

3. Swinton and Mowat, *Practical Theology and Qualitative Research*, 5–6.
4. Keener, *Spirit Hermeneutics*, 25–26.

its way into the creases of one's being. It is just like when my son leaves his toy figurines out in the back yard for too long: the dirt becomes imbedded and gets into all the joints and cracks.

Chris Green also noticed the danger in how the church divides identity and purpose in its preaching. He says that dividing it in this way separates our "being" from our "doing," which suggests that the first (i.e., identity) is more important than the second (i.e., purpose). Green insists this causes more trouble than what it is worth. His solution is to change the dynamic. So, rather than a linear approach of our identity leading to our purpose and calling (or "vocation" as Green calls it), our identity and vocation are, instead, codependent and equally rooted in the life of Christ. Both unfold as we join with Christ in his vocation and mission.

Green's approach is firmly rooted in the Trinity. He explains how for each of the Trinity members, the way that they operate in creation reveals their identity to us.[5] For instance, although John the Baptist was reluctant to baptize Jesus, Jesus explained he needed John to baptize him in order to fulfill all righteousness (Matt 3:15). Immediately after, the Father identified Jesus as his son (Matt 3:17). In one swoop, God affirmed Jesus' identity and announced his vocation.[6] The same holds for the Holy Spirit. We know him by his works (John 10:38). Green then applies this logic to us as believers, and he says that we know ourselves (our identity) only as we walk in the light as Jesus is in the light (our vocation). Therefore, our identity and vocation are rooted in the life that we have in Christ, and identity and vocation are codependent, so we do not have to establish one in order to find the other. Instead, both unfold as we live each day in the life and light of Christ.[7]

Derek Prince, who was one of the Charismatic movement's most prominent Bible teachers in the twentieth-century, makes a good point in his biography. His biographer asked if Prince had any driving ambition or dream for the future. Prince responded, "I can honestly say I had a total lack of ambition. I don't mean to say I had no hope or spiritual passion. I simply had no ambition. As for destiny. I think that is a word used today as a substitute for kingdom building or the drive for power."

His biographer asked, "But don't you believe that men are made for a purpose?"

---

5. Green, *Sanctifying Interpretation*, 8–10.

6. Green, *Sanctifying Interpretation*, 11–12.

7. Green, *Sanctifying Interpretation*, 12–15.

"Yes, but that purpose is to know the Lord. The meaning of life is relationship. The future comes from pursuing Him, not pursuing the future."[8]

For me, Christianity's linear approach to preaching identity and purpose misses the mark. It focuses on "who I am" and "what I must do." But, if we see our identity and vocation as part of Christ's life, the focus is less about us and more about Christ. As Prince says, "The future comes from pursuing Him, not pursuing the future." In this, our lives naturally unfold as we live in the light of Christ. If we apply this to depression, we see that depression's adverse effects—how it negatively affects the sufferer's identity and purpose and prevents them from experiencing God—all take place within the life and security of Christ (1 Cor 10:13). As with us all, sometimes meaninglessness may immerse us and push us down, but we stand because we died, and our life is hidden with Christ in God (Col 3:3).

---

8. Mansfield, *Derek Prince: A Biography*, 169.

7

The Church's Silence

THE CHURCH'S SILENCE

NOT ONCE DURING MY second bout of depression did I consider speaking to any member of my church's leadership or pastoral care staff for help. I never even told my friends. The only person who knew was my wife, and she only knew because she saw me struggling. This inaction on my part corresponds to results from the survey that I conducted years later as a doctoral student in the USA. In the survey, I asked two questions to depression sufferers within Pentecostal churches. The first question asked what they thought of their home church's pastoral care team, church community, and friends in supporting them in their struggle with depression. Approximately 50 percent of respondents said that they had not told any of them. This was an interesting observation considering that the same question showed that approximately 35 percent of sufferers who told their pastoral care team or community and their friends found them to be supportive. The second question I asked was, "If you never told your current church friends of your depression, what stopped you?" Twenty percent responded that it was their private concern, and a further 21 percent said that there was no one close enough in the church to whom they could talk. On another question, 44 percent of the respondents said they were ashamed of their depression.[1] I understood these responses to mean that local churches could help people

---

1. McBain, "Exploring the Silent Nature of Depression," 116–23.

with depression, but because depression sufferers were not speaking out, in some ways, they were not allowing their churches to help.

Sometimes I ask myself why I did not tell my church friends or the pastoral care team about my battle with depression. I do not think that I was ashamed. If I was to hazard a guess: what stopped me from telling others was my belief that it was my personal issue that I was responsible for handling alone. As with so many others, depression silenced me. Nevertheless, would I have internalized it if my home church talked about mental health and depression? I do not know. I cannot remember if my home church in the UK, back then, ever approached the topic. I can only speculate that if they tackled mental health issues, I might have opened up and discussed my struggle with the pastoral care team or my friends in the church community. Maybe others struggling in silence would have opened up too. Who knows? However, I do not think that what I experienced from my church or how I internalized my illness and did not speak of it was any different from the experiences of many others struggling with mental health and depression.

Amy Simpson is a Christian author and mental health advocate who has had her own experiences with mental illness and the church. She describes the church's stigma of mental illness, and she criticizes its silence as isolating and cruel. She says that the church handles mental illness in ways that do not show the love of God.[2] Heather Vacek describes how stigma and fear promotes silence and avoidance in the church.[3] LifeWay's extensive survey found that few churches are talking to their members about mental illness. Generally, a survey of the voices that are speaking on the issue reveals a culture of stigma and silence in the church that leads to shame.[4] This may be true, but the church did not always respond in this way. In the past, the church was at the center of healthcare and healing, including depression and mental health.

THE CHURCH'S HISTORY WITH DEPRESSION

History knows depression as "melancholia," which is a term taken from the Latin transliteration of a Greek word that refers to a condition that

---

2. Simpson, "Mental Illness: What Is the Church's Role?"
3. Vacek, *Madness*, 3.
4. LifeWay Research, "New Study of Acute Mental illness and Christian Faith."

involved prolonged sadness, fear, and depression.[5] The earliest references to melancholia are from ancient Mesopotamian literature dating from 2000 BC. Sources describe how people back then thought that demonic possession caused all mental illnesses, which meant that although physicians were available to perform physical treatments, they considered melancholia to be a spiritual illness. Hence, treatment was the responsibility of the priests. In the fifth century BC, Hippocrates identified the symptoms of melancholy as persistent sadness and morbid thoughts. He thought that imbalances in bodily humors caused melancholy. The four humors referred to the theory that there were four unique kinds of bodily fluids present within the human body: yellow bile, black bile, phlegm, and blood. Imbalances of these humors could cause emotional and temperamental changes. Hippocrates believed that too much black bile caused melancholia, so his cure involved bathing, exercising, dieting, and bloodletting.[6]

Bloodletting is an ancient technique that involves draining blood from the patient and was a go-to medical treatment up to the twentieth century. It is still used today for certain conditions. Perhaps the most common type of bloodletting currently, although we might not think of it as such, is donating blood. I find it interesting how historically they used bloodletting as a medical treatment for melancholia because it compares with self-harm. Yes, there are vast differences in many respects. A depressed person's motivation to self-harm is assumed to be an act of self-hatred and a call for help. In contrast, bloodletting is a medical approach that is built upon a specific theory of knowledge. In the most basic sense, though, I see a comparison with how both activities involve the simple act of breaking the skin to release blood and, thereby, making the person feel better.

Although there was a variety of opinions among the Romans about what caused melancholy—with some thinking demons caused it and others believing it was a biological and psychological disease—Hippocrates' idea that melancholia was biological seems to have held the preeminent position.[7] For instance, both Galen and Aretaeus, who wrote in the first century AD, considered it an affliction of the brain.[8] However, as Hippocrates' influence faded, melancholia's biological causes fell out of favor among the Romans. They came to typically believe that demons or that

---

5. Blazer, *The Age of Melancholy*, 46.
6. Nemade, et al., "Historical Understandings of Depression."
7. Nemade, et al., "Historical Understandings of Depression."
8. Taylor and Fink, *Melancholia*, 2.

being the focus of a god's anger caused melancholia. Cornelius Celsus (25 BC–50 AD) advocated starvation, shackles, and beatings as treatments.[9] Thank goodness that worldviews change!

After the fall of the Roman empire in the fifth century and Christianity becoming the dominant religion, most people thought that demon possession, the devil, or witches caused mental illness. The typical treatment was exorcism or the punishment and execution of the witch in question. Even then, a minority of physicians still believed that imbalanced humors or some other biological abnormalities caused melancholia and other mental illnesses. This minority opinion persisted during the Middle Ages and leading up to the Protestant Reformation and Counter-Reformation. Allison Coudert discusses this period (i.e., the early modern period, roughly 1500 to 1800). She says there was a growing consensus during this period that demonic possession caused melancholy and other forms of mental illness, which religion and doctrine played a considerable role in developing.[10] She argues that an attitude of uncertainty prevailed in Europe around the Catholic Church's ability to provide a clear route of salvation. Martin Luther responded to this in his Ninety-Five Theses. He believed that he could help reform the Catholic Church; over time, though, his rhetoric took on a much harsher tone, dramatizing the role of Satan and demons in world affairs and their war against humans.[11] The contest between Christians and demons is typical of church history and is nothing new. For example, the fear of evil was rife in Late Antiquity (c. 200 AD–700 AD). During that period, any pagan or Christian could readily point to an unfortunate event or illness as evidence of demonic activity. People from every class level considered Christian ascetics and monks as potent healers of demonic possession through their power to handle demons successfully.[12]

Two things seem to have happened during the Reformation and shortly afterward. First, the Reformers emphasized the role of Satan and demons in human life and how life was one long struggle against the demonic. Second, they mixed this view with Martin Luther's and John Calvin's belief that humanity was so depraved and sinful that only God's grace could save people. The combination of both of these things broadcast human nature in a very dim light that brought about anxiety, alienation, and self-loathing, which

---

9. Nemade, et al., "Historical Understandings of Depression."
10. Coudert, "Melancholy, Madness, and Demonic Possession," 563.
11. Coudert, "Melancholy, Madness, and Demonic Possession," 654.
12. Iosif, "I Saw Satan Fall like Lightning from Heaven," 323–24.

fostered an epidemic of madness and melancholy.[13] Coudert explains how those Christians living before the Protestant Reformation once enjoyed the support of priests, saints, and the Virgin Mary as spiritual intercessors against the marauding demons. However, the Reformers removed these intercessors from their belief system, which meant that Christians now had to fend for themselves when battling on the frontline against Satan and his minions. This caused further uncertainty and anxiety among the masses, which, when mixed with the people's perception of nothingness and worthlessness, augmented an already fragile melancholic state. Because of this and the cultural belief that demons infested the world, people of this period thought that demonic possession caused melancholy and madness.[14] The church's response to these beliefs was exorcism.

Over the centuries, exorcists and theologians published various texts that detailed methods and provided instructions on how to identify demonic possession. As these texts developed, so did different symptoms of demon possession. As an example, the reputable exorcist Girolamo Menghi (1529–1609) described the following as signs of demon possession:

1. Speaking a foreign language previously unknown.
2. Revealing secrets and predicting the future.
3. Showing unnatural physical strength.
4. Exhibiting hatred toward priests and holy objects.
5. Sinking into melancholy and desperation.
6. Exploding in anger and uttering blasphemies.
7. Vomiting sharp objects such as knives and glass.[15]

With so many people writing about possession and exorcism, it was inevitable that conflicting symptoms emerged. In response to these differences, the texts encouraged exorcists to seek a physician's opinion before performing an exorcism. They hoped that a medical professional's advice would weed out frauds and stop mistakes from happening.[16]

The development of conflicting symptoms and appeals to medical professionals within the literature reveal a tension between two competing

---

13. Coudert, "Melancholy, Madness, and Demonic Possession," 655–56.
14. Coudert, "Melancholy, Madness, and Demonic Possession," 653—58.
15. Coudert. "Melancholy, Madness, and Demonic Possession," 663.
16. Coudert, "Melancholy, Madness, and Demonic Possession," 664–66.

The Church's Silence

worldviews. On one side was a spiritual understanding of the world that people were increasingly questioning. On the other side was a developing rationalistic worldview that was based on reductionism and reason. A transition was taking place between Medieval and Enlightenment cosmology. Before the Enlightenment, the following hierarchy made up Medieval cosmology, in descending order: God, the church, the monarch and nobles, people, animals, plants, and objects. Within this hierarchy, humans looked upward to the monarch, nobles, the church, and God for meaning and purpose in their lives. As the Enlightenment developed, it eradicated the levels of God, church, monarch, and nobility. People ceased to look upward for life's meaning and purpose, and they looked downward to animals, plants, and objects.[17] Empiricist and positivist models of understanding emerged that relied heavily on reductionism. Exclusivity developed, which did not consider the reality of anything that was not rationally explainable, i.e., the existence of demons or any spiritual dynamic. The emergence of this new enlightened worldview meant that exorcism was no longer the proper response to mental health issues, including depression. As a point of interest, I should add that there has been a recent resurgence in exorcism, especially among Pentecostals and Charismatics. Even the Catholic Church updated its exorcism manual in 1999—its first update since 1614. One Catholic priest recently claimed to have conducted 70,000 exorcisms.[18] This number is not a typo!

Blazer mentions that although theological explanations for melancholy eclipsed much of Europe, the view that the bodily humors caused melancholy persisted, and alchemical (i.e., chemical) theories emerged that relied on the use of early medicines for treatment.[19] Robert Burton (1577–1640), an English Anglican priest, wrote substantially about melancholy in his book *The Anatomy of Melancholy* (1621). He saw it as primarily a disease with a physiological cause within which the bodily humors played an important role. Burton's approach was not one-dimensional. He left room for other explanations, and he developed what Blazer refers to as a "multi-causal web" of explanations. These included the effects of life experiences (like death, loss, and poverty), physical injury (like blows to the head), biological disorders, heredity factors, and health-related behaviors. Naturally, Burton also left room for God and the devil in his model. He

---

17. Bosch, *Transforming Mission*, 263.
18. Levack, "The Horrors of Witchcraft and Demonic Possession," 931–32.
19. Blazer, *The Age of Melancholy*, 41–42.

wrote a chapter on religious melancholy that he based upon the cultural understanding of the late Renaissance that melancholy was a malady that visited someone because he or she had departed from God.[20]

Coudert observes that people of this period, including Burton, believed that the devil caused religious melancholy by luring them and snaring them into sin, which then led to disease, death, and damnation.[21] In a period when religion influenced culture, such an explanation was viable. Even into the eighteenth and nineteenth centuries, the Protestant understanding of humanity painted such a bleak picture that people could not be sure whether they were in or out of God's plan. Anxiety, doubt, and despair abounded, and many people had their "dark nights of the soul." Blazer argues that escape from this came through the religious enthusiasm of the Great Awakenings, as well as subsequent revivals and social movements that spread throughout America during the Industrial Age of the eighteenth and nineteenth centuries.[22]

As the Great Awakenings and religious enthusiasm moved across America, physicians slowly separated madness from religion. The Enlightenment brought a more medicalized view that coincided with a positive understanding of humanity that was different from the sinful beings that the Reformers broadcast. A change took place from the seventeenth century, in which thinkers gave preeminence to the power of reason. Human reason had the power to make humanity good or bad. Sin had nothing to do with it. Modern melancholy developed upon an understanding of self-awareness and a growing sense of individuality.

Coudert describes the freedoms that urbanization brought during this period. Those who moved to the cities from rural areas remade themselves and pursued lifestyles that were free from the restraints placed upon them by their birth, family background, and social status. There was a growing sense of freedom and individuality in the city that people expressed through the solitary past-times of letter-writing, diary-keeping, and reading, all of which fostered internal reflection and a growing sense of individuality. This increasing sense of individuality meant that people ceased interpreting depression and mental illness by using a social context, and they began interpreting it from their individual contexts. This "anthropological revolution" brought many new personal freedoms, which brought with them their

---

20. Blazer, *The Age of Melancholy*, 42–45.
21. Coudert, "Melancholy, Madness, and Demonic Possession," 661.
22. Blazer, *The Age of Melancholy*, 46.

own set of anxieties, fears, and pressures to conform to the new ideals of decorum, politeness, and civility, which, although less constraining, were no less potent than those that they replaced.[23]

During this period, the theology of madness gave way to the medicalization of madness, which then gave rise to the psychology of madness, so that by the end of the eighteenth century, most people understood that madness was a natural malady and it had nothing to do with God or the supernatural.[24] Over time, people understood religious melancholy as a "pathological psychological" condition, and it was medicalized. As mentioned, this medicalization came hand-in-hand with a more positive view of humanity. Patients preferred a more physical explanation of what was bothering them because it minimized their personal responsibility, guilt, and shame.[25] As Christianity entered the twentieth century, religious melancholy (i.e., depression) as a reaction to God faded as culture changed to celebrate the freedom of the individual.[26]

In the nineteenth century, physicians recognized melancholia as a core illness among many forms of insanity. During this time, disagreements on what to call psychiatric disorders led to attempts to develop standardized terminology.[27] Emil Kraepelin distinguished manic depression (i.e., bipolar disorder) from dementia (i.e., schizophrenia).[28] He believed that depression was an abnormal mood state caused by a core mental disorder.[29] On the contrary, Sigmund Freud theorized that melancholia was a

---

23. Coudert, "Melancholy, Madness, and Demonic Possession," 679–80, referencing Terry Castle, "The Culture of Travesty: Sexuality and Masquerade in Eighteenth-Century England," in *British Literature, 1640-1789: A Critical Reader*, edited by Robert Demaria Jr., (Oxford: Blackwell, 1999), 251–70; Daniel Shanahan, *Toward a Genealogy of Individualism* (Amherst, MA: University of Massachusetts, 1992); Jerrold E. Seigel, *The Idea of the Self: Thought and Experience in Western Europe* (Cambridge: Cambridge University Press, 2005); Norbert Elias, *The Civilizing Process*, translated by Edmund Jephcott, 1939. (Oxford, UK: Blackwell, 2000); Wolfgang Weber, "Im Kampf mit Saturn: Zur Bedeutung der Melancholie im an- thropologischen Modernisierungsprozess des 16. und 17. Jahrhunderts," *Zeitschrift für historische Forschung* 17 (1990) 155–92; David M. Turner, *Fashioning Adultery: Gender, Sex and Civility in England, 1660–1740* (Cambridge, UK: Cambridge University Press, 2002).
24. Coudert, "Melancholy, Madness, and Demonic Possession," 650–51.
25. Coudert, "Melancholy, Madness, and Demonic Possession," 678.
26. Blazer, *The Age of Melancholy*, 46.
27. Taylor and Fink, *Melancholia*, 3–4.
28. Schimelpfening, "The History of Depression."
29. Taylor and Fink, *Melancholia*, 6–8.

response to real or symbolic loss. He believed that unconscious anger over the loss led to self-hatred and self-destructive behavior. He believed that psychoanalysis could help a person resolve these unconscious conflicts, thereby reducing self-destructive thoughts and behaviors. Other doctors during this time followed in the footsteps of Kraepelin and saw depression as a brain disorder.[30] They understood that depression had biological origins and required biological treatment.[31] This approach met with resistance among Freud and his followers, whose ideas, Taylor and Fink argue, would not have gained so much traction had there been a competing biological model of psychiatric illness with effective treatment available.[32] However, as the twentieth century progressed, pharmaceutical effectiveness in treating other mental ailments meant that a new optimism arose for seeing depression as a biological illness with a psychiatric cure.[33] In 1950, doctors noticed that a tuberculosis medication called isoniazid seemed helpful in treating depression in some people. Therefore, doctors looked at drug therapies for treatment, whereas before, the only remedy was psychotherapy.[34]

As pharmaceuticals became more effective in treating depression, scientists increasingly saw it as a biological illness.[35] This understanding of depression came to permeate much of the health system through the biomedical model. The biomedical model is a healthcare model that views humans as machines and disease as a dysfunction that we must control, minimize, or eliminate.[36] Within this model, how a patient experiences depression is a symptom of the biological abnormality itself.[37] This model, linked with the success of new medications and the pharmaceutical industry's influence, came to define and interpret depression.[38] This move completely took mental illness and depression out of the church's domain, and firmly placed it within the medical domain. This shift in professionalization meant that the medical sector monopolized the physical and mental aspects of healing. At the same time, the clergy gave up their position as providers

---

30. Schimelpfening, "The History of Depression."
31. Blazer, *The Age of Melancholy*, 39.
32. Taylor and Fink, *Melancholia*, 6.
33. Taylor and Fink, *Melancholia*, 7.
34. Schimelpfening, "The History of Depression."
35. Taylor and Fink, *Melancholia*, 7.
36. Swinton, "Healing Presence," 68–69.
37. Engel, "The Need for a New Medical Model," 39.
38. Blazer, *The Age of Melancholy*, 11.

of care for mental ailments.[39] The clergy lost their voice, and people no longer saw them as experts. Silence and avoidance, promoted by stigma and fear,[40] or referral, became the church's modus operandi.

CHAPTER SUMMARY

A more in-depth historical investigation into church history would show that the church has had more responses than those we discussed and would offer various theological workings behind those responses. Still, one aim of this historical survey was to show how depression is contextual. What causes depression, how someone experiences it, who that person goes to for treatment, and the treatment methods that are utilized, all are dependent upon worldview. As Hester E. Oberman says, "Mental health is dependent upon our belief system."[41] Some of depression's symptoms are timeless and are experienced the same cross-culturally, but people also experience depression in a way that is consistent with their social and cultural contexts.[42]

Considering that "illness represents personal, interpersonal, and cultural reactions to disease or discomfort,"[43] an interaction takes place within each patient that helps them interpret their experience of depression in a way that is consistent with their culture. A person's expectations, values, hopes, culture, and worldview are mediums that make up a person's life experiences, and these teach the person how to respond to pain. These factors further contribute to the meaning that a person places on their suffering.[44] Because of this, a twentieth-century American will experience illness and approach treatment in a way that is consistent with their culture. This American's approach will be different from how a fifteenth-century European would have experienced their illness and approached treatment. The dominant worldview and culture, of which both people are a part, will govern their experiences, their interpretations of those experiences, who they go to for help, and their treatment.

---

39. Vacek, *Madness*, 3.
40. Vacek, *Madness*, 3.
41. Oberman, "A Postmodern Perspective," 690.
42. Fenton and Sadiq-Sangster, "Culture, Relativism and the Expression of Mental Distress," 67–68.
43. Kleinman, et al., "Culture, Illness, and Care," 141.
44. Swinton, "Healing Presence," 68–69.

Likewise, the church responds to depression, as with other illnesses, in ways that are consistent with its context. For someone in twelfth-century Europe who is experiencing melancholy, the church's response may be an exorcism. For someone living in eighteenth-century America, the church's reaction may be to interpret that person's experience by using religious melancholy or through the religious enthusiasm of the Great Awakenings. And the church's response is different again today. As our culture and worldview changed throughout the twentieth century, the cause of depression moved from being spiritual to biological. Treatment moved into the realm of the medical profession. This move coincided with broader cultural transformations, and health became a private matter between the patient and their doctor, thus excluding the clergy. These responses correspond to the beliefs of the dominant worldview of the period. For each of those responses, changes in worldview govern the usefulness of the response.

These findings help explain why the church's current response to the issue of depression is one of silence. The church is silent because western culture has taught it to be. The church responds to depression in ways that are consistent with its current context. Likewise, the local church of which I was a member in the UK for four years never spoke about depression or mental health because culture told it not to speak. Those issues were personal, between doctor and patient, and the local church had nothing to offer anybody in that area.

8

The Church's Response

OUR CULTURE IS CHANGING in such a way that it opens avenues for the church to have a positive impact on the lives of those suffering from depression and other mental health issues. Like a tag-line for a movie poster, Oberman argues that despite being sidelined throughout most of the twentieth century, religion has "resurface[d] with a vengeance" and proves to be a formative force in the framework of mental health.[1] Helen L. Leathard's views are similar. She describes how the biomedical model reduced the church's idea of healing to standing at a distance and offering prayers of intercession. However, the recent resurgence of the ministry of healing has returned the church to the discussion. The ministry of healing, Leathard says, is a journey towards wholeness. It encompasses both a spiritual and natural dynamic that includes the restoration of relationships within society.[2] This chapter will discuss Christian hospitality and friendship as one option available for the church to offer the restorative and formative force of healing to depressed people within our society and communities. Through hospitality and friendship, the church can find its place in today's changing culture by fulfilling its role as the Body of Christ as it operates as a redeemed community that brings wholeness to the broken.

---

1. Oberman, "A Postmodern Perspective," 690–91.
2. Leathard, "Healing in the Christian Tradition," 33–34.

HOSPITALITY AND FRIENDSHIP

Whenever we meet an unfamiliar person, we use our social norms to judge whether they are "one of us." If we recognize that they are "one of us," then we feel comfortable with them and include them. However, if we judge the person as "other," then our natural response is to stereotype and categorize them as different and to stay away from them. This results in stigma, because their attributes vary from our society's expectations. In this process we are judging them according to their "virtual social identity." Virtual social identity looks at the outside of a person to see if they fit in, whereas "actual social identity" looks at the inside of the person to see if they are acceptable. We can compare the concepts of social and virtual identity to what God said to the prophet Samuel, "Do not look at his appearance or at his physical stature, because I have refused him. For *the* Lord does not see as man sees; for man looks at the outward appearance, but the Lord looks at the heart" (1 Sam 16:7). As this relates to us, our natural inclination may be to stay away from a man who looks "weird" (virtual social identity), but unknown to us, the man may be a gracious person and a proper philanthropist (actual social identity). The takeaway element is that first impressions may be deceiving. Generally, though, we tend to label those who do not fit into our social norms as "the other" and different. Therefore, stigma surfaces in human relationships when a person's attributes vary from what society says they should be. Stigma drives a wedge between us, and the visibility of the stigmatizing traits determines the impact.[3]

Depression tends to have non-visible traits, so sufferers often go undetected in our midst and are less prone to being stigmatized. We probably meet people every day, both inside and outside the church, who are depressed. They look the same as us, they act the same as us, and, for all intents and purposes, they are the same as us; yet they struggle with depression. Such people avoid external labeling, but just because the effects of their illness are not visible does not mean that they avoid labeling altogether. For a depressed person, as with any mentally ill person, labeling begins in the doctor's office. We noted previously that in today's medicalized culture, which sees disease as a biological dysfunction, we respond to disease as something that we must control or eliminate to function in society. Therefore, as soon as someone receives a diagnosis, although only they and the doctor know, they still receive the label of someone who does

---

3. Vacek, *Madness*, 165.

not meet society's norms. The doctor further enforces the patient's label and dysfunction because the doctor assumes that if specific controls are in place (i.e., prescription medicine), then the movement towards mental healing can begin.[4] Therefore, the medicalized treatment of the mental illness reinforces the label.

Labeling, Swinton says, means that the person loses their personal identity. So, when someone receives the diagnosis of depression, they become a "depressive." This label acts as a cultural lens through which the sufferer interprets every life experience.[5] Media plays an enormous part in labeling and stigmatizing, because it portrays people with mental illness and depression as the "other."[6] Therefore, when sufferers go to church, they may see themselves as those whom others will stigmatize. This means that sufferers will navigate church life differently than those who do not have that label.[7] Since assumptions about mental illness usually are negative, depression sufferers tend to exclude themselves from the community.[8] In many respects, depressed people stigmatize themselves. Therefore, stigmatization takes two forms. On one hand, sufferers stigmatize themselves, and on the other hand, the church stigmatizes sufferers. Paralysis exists on both sides.

Further compounding matters is the fact that those with depression feel detached from those closest to them. Depression sufferers think no one understands what they are going through and no one can relate to them. It is natural for people suffering and in pain to feel this way because suffering is unique to each person and is filled with deep individual meaning. Swinton proposes that suffering and the personal significance of illness depend on historical and relationship factors that are known only to the sufferer. A person's expectations, values, hopes, culture, and worldview are mediums that make up a person's life experiences and teach them how to respond to pain. These factors further contribute to the meaning that a person places on the event(s) that caused their suffering and pain.[9] Isolation, therefore, is a somewhat justified response, because sufferers are correct in their assessment that "No one knows what's going on inside me, or how I feel."

---

4. Swinton, "Healing Presence," 70.
5. Swinton, "Healing Presence," 72–73.
6. Vacek, *Madness*, 166.
7. Vacek, *Madness*, 167.
8. Swinton, "Healing Presence," 72–73.
9. Swinton, "Healing Presence," 68–69.

Stanley Hauerwas insists that those in pain want help, and those not in pain want to help. However, it is difficult for those not in pain to help, because they cannot experience the sufferings of others. This dilemma causes a double burden, because it is difficult enough making friends with strangers at church when everything is normal—never mind when pain is present.[10] The difficulty with depression, though, is that sufferers rarely mention their suffering. Onlookers may think that a depressed person is healthy, but inside they are in pain dealing with exclusion and isolation issues. Therefore, the shared experience of pain is essential in friendship. Even then, no matter how sympathetic the other party might be, only shared pain of a particular kind and source provides a shared experience. Otherwise, pain isolates people from one another, and it also separates the person in distress from themselves, because they hesitate to admit they are in pain. After all, admission makes them feel vulnerable.[11]

The stigma of depression and the pain that it causes demand a response. It is sad, though, that sometimes just thinking about how to respond is enough to put people off responding.[12] Still, hospitality is perhaps one of the church's most innate responses, because Jesus provides our best example for friendship. His approach differs from how our society sees friendship. Our society understands friendship in ways that are self-serving, individualistic, and shallow. However, Jesus structured his approach to friendship through grace and love. He befriended those who were unlike him. Cultural assumptions did not constrain Jesus by telling him with whom to fellowship. He was available to those whom society marginalized and stigmatized, and those whom the religious system refused access to God.[13]

The Good News of Jesus is an invitation to those outside God's household to enter and take a seat at God's table. As Elizabeth Barnes puts it, the faith community is a household that invites people to take part in Christ's story by entering Christ's house. The invitation goes out to the lame, the outcast, the weak, and the infirm, all of whom find strength and identity by joining with the faith community in Christ's story.[14] The gospel and Christian friendship defy social norms. They draw people together into mutual

---

10. Hauerwas, *Suffering Presence*, 80–81.
11. Hauerwas, *Suffering Presence*, 79–80.
12. Hauerwas, *Suffering Presence*, 80–81.
13. Swinton, "Healing Presence," 72–74.
14. Barnes, *The Story of Discipleship*, 45.

relationships with one another and God, thus reorienting people within society,[15] while providing friendship by being present amid the pain.[16] Swinton says that having meaningful friendships contributes to one's healing more than clinical treatment alone, because friendships support spiritual and psychological health. Friendships do this by giving people a sense of identity and an awareness of their value, meaning, and purpose, within which friendship with God provides the ultimate significance.[17]

HOSPITALITY AND SPACE

Perhaps one of the most considerable challenges in being hospitable and developing friendships like Jesus is how to facilitate these types of friendships within the local church community. This is especially true when we recognize that it is the suffering from a particular kind and source that provides a shared experience.[18] Nevertheless, the task falls to church communities to provide the physical and spiritual space where Christlike friendship can occur, and where those who are "different" can find a home.[19] This is what hospitality is: it is a physical and spiritual space amid the stigma, suffering, and pain, through which flows Jesus' style of friendship. The fact is, though, that if we knew the full stories of some people in our church communities, our knee-jerk reaction would be to assume that we lack the necessary skills to befriend them. Our inadequacies and shortcomings may be legitimate, but if we are not careful, then these become vehicles for us to hide our prejudices and stigmatizing labels. We must abandon this attitude, because it prevents us from knowing those who are suffering. To help us, Swinton suggests creating "safe spaces" within the church for people to develop friendships.[20]

There is a close association between healing and space. Everything that takes place around us, along with how we position ourselves when something challenges our norms, values, and beliefs, determine our healthiness and the extent of healing in our lives.[21] Louw says that incarnational and

---

15. Vacek, *Madness*, 161–62.
16. Hauerwas, *Suffering Presence*, 80–81.
17. Swinton, "Healing Presence," 70–71.
18. Hauerwas, *Suffering Presence*, 79–80.
19. Swinton, "Healing Presence," 74–75.
20. Swinton, "Healing Presence," 74–75.
21. Louw, "Space and Place in the Healing of Life," 427.

eschatological concepts contribute towards and help develop spaces and areas. The Holy Spirit plays a vital role in this, because he indwells Christians with God's presence. Therefore, Christians act as the incarnational Body of Christ in the spaces and places where they find themselves.[22] In this sense, when we speak of creating safe spaces within the church where friendships can develop, we are talking about spaces and places where God's people carry God's presence and where the Holy Spirit is present to help facilitate Jesus-style friendships. These friendships address the ontological issues that affect the status and identity of humans. They also include an eschatological understanding of humanity by seeing humans as beings who live in response to Jesus' death and resurrection. Within such friendships, people find a home "where there is neither Jew nor Greek, male nor female, mentally ill nor mentally healthy, but only travelers struggling together to sustain faith in God and trust in one another."[23]

These spaces can take many forms and include everything from using the church's spare room for a Sunday School class or a Wednesday night cell group, to using the church's parking lot as a drive-in food bank. Even social media or meeting for coffee acts as spaces. There is an infinite amount of spaces through which church communities can show Jesus-style friendships. Perhaps the most obvious and convenient is the worship service. Swinton observes how acts of worship, formal or informal, bind the sufferer to the church community. Therefore, although the depression sufferer may intellectually have given up their belief in God and hope of healing, their position within the church binds them to the community and provides them the momentum they need to continue on their journey. An example that Swinton provides is of one lady who describes how the church's worship service acts as a safe space where she can bring her doubts and questions to God within the comfort of a community of fellow worshipers. The preaching, symbolism, music, and lyrics provide her with a medium that goes beyond the restrictions placed upon her by her doubting mind and help her express her deep longings to God and her spiritual need. Through the church service, she can believe, despite her struggles.[24]

---

22. Louw, "Space and Place in the Healing of Life," 434–38.
23. Swinton, "Healing Presence," 74–75.
24. Swinton, *Spirituality and Mental Health Care*, 128–29.

SANCTIFICATION WITHIN FAITH COMMUNITIES

Our considerations on hospitality and friendship naturally lead us to reflect upon the role sanctification plays within faith communities. The word "sanctification" means "set apart" or "consecrated." William Menzies describes it as "an act of separation from that which is evil and of dedication unto God (Rom. 12:1–2; 1 Thess. 5:23; Heb. 13:12)."[25] Anthony Thiselton explains that in the New Testament, sanctification is the *"long and gradual process of becoming* holy, or like Christ." The Spirit nurtures in us such qualities as love, patience, kindness, gentleness, faithfulness, soundness of mind, and other positive attributes that are characteristic of a lifestyle pleasing to God (Gal 5:22–23).[26] Menzies says that God is not only concerned with outward obedience to his will, but he also wants purity and cleanliness in the inward wellspring of our motivation (cf. Mark 7:6; Luke 6:45). Menzies writes, "As the light of God's Spirit and Word floods the heart and mind, the believer is expected to respond, cooperating with God by removing himself from defilement (2 Cor. 7:1; Heb. 12:13–15)."[27]

The New Testament writers did not primarily author their works to individuals but to faith communities. Robert Jewett explains how much modern literature focuses on the Spirit's role in sanctifying individuals, yet Jewett argues that the Spirit consecrates through the community. Holiness, in the collective sense, refers to the transformation of social life. The Spirit transforms, converts, and maintains purity among the faith community, within and through which he operates.[28] So, when Paul, in his letter to the Galatians, tells us to walk in the Spirit and not fulfill the lusts of the flesh (Gal 5:16), he is not only saying this for our individual benefit, but for the benefit of the entire church community. With the community in mind, the works of the flesh (Gal 5:19–21) are problematic—not just because they are ungodly and represent a lifestyle that we Christians must avoid, but also because they are anti-social and weaken the faith community. As Thiselton says, "[The apostle] Paul makes clear that absence of the work of the Holy Spirit leads to anti-social qualities."[29]

---

25. Menzies, *Bible Doctrines: A Pentecostal Perspective*, 146.
26. Thiselton, *A Shorter Guide to the Holy Spirit*, 117.
27. Menzies, *Bible Doctrines: A Pentecostal Perspective*, 149.
28. Jewett, *Romans: A Commentary*, 908.
29. Thiselton, *A Shorter Guide to the Holy Spirit*, 118.

When we consider depression's effectiveness at isolating sufferers from the community in contrast to how the Spirit nurtures the community, it is logical to see the Spirit's sanctifying role within and through the church community as a means of healing from depression. This is especially true when we consider that the characteristics of depression (i.e., apathy, weakness, sadness, despair, etc.) are all contrary to the characteristics of the Christian life (i.e., love, abiding peace, soundness of mind, joy, etc.). Therefore, how we demonstrate our faith is essential if we are to reach out and journey with depression sufferers to wholeness. The apostle James discussed this in James 2:14–24:

> What does it profit, my brethren, if someone says he has faith but does not have works? Can faith save him? If a brother or sister is naked and destitute of daily food, and one of you says to them, "Depart in peace, be warmed and filled," but you do not give them the things which are needed for the body, what does it profit? Thus also faith by itself, if it does not have works, is dead.
>
> But someone will say, "You have faith, and I have works." Show me your faith without your works, and I will show you my faith by my works. You believe that there is one God. You do well. Even the demons believe—and tremble! But do you want to know, O foolish man, that faith without works is dead?

This passage explains that our faith is dead unless it produces good works. James sees it this way: there is a saving faith that leads to good works, and there is a dead non-saving faith that does not lead to good works. For James, faith and works go hand-in-hand. Peter Davids says, "Both are important and must equally be present or else the other alone is 'worthless,' just as body and spirit are each 'worthless' when separated from one another."[30]

The apostle James is making these comments concerning faith and works within a community where materially prosperous individuals, who confess faith in Jesus, are not helping those in need. According to James, those materially solvent believers may confess faith and be supporters of the faith, but they do not possess a faith that saves them, for their acts of mercy would show if they had saving faith.[31] For James, saving faith is a trusting faith that flows into deeds of mercy, whereas non-saving faith is creedal faith without deeds of mercy. In this setting, James can distinguish faith from works to argue that "Faith finds its perfection and fulfillment

---

30. Davids, *The Epistle of James*, 123.
31. McKnight, *The Letter of James*, 124.

in acts of mercy."[32] There is a similarity here with what the apostle Paul says in Galatians 5:6, "For in Christ Jesus neither circumcision nor uncircumcision counts for anything; the only thing that counts is faith working through love."[33]

In some respects, what we are talking about here concerning the demonstration of saving faith through acts of mercy is mission. Trevor Burke describes how God has given us a relational Spirit and has made us part of a relational community,[34] the output of which is mission.[35] Menzies, commenting on Titus 2:11–14, says that sanctification carries with it a powerful sense of dedication in the way that God desires those whom he redeems to consecrate themselves for his worship and service.[36] Worship and service are outgrowths of sanctification. Because the faith community demonstrates sanctification as acts of mercy, the local church takes on a missional role through which it is responsible to reach out to those who suffer and to walk with them toward wholeness.

SUMMARY

The demonstration of the believer's sanctification through faith practices within the church community can enrich their experiences of suffering by providing meaning. Human experience reveals that suffering is vibrant and unique to each of us and is filled with personal meaning beyond any physical or psychological symptoms that we experience as part of our suffering. Neither can we describe suffering only in terms of pain or assess it on a universal scale. Suffering and the personal meaning of illness depend on historical and relationship factors known only to the sufferer. A person's expectations, values, hopes, culture, and worldview are mediums that make up a person's life experiences and teach the person how to respond to pain. These factors help sufferers see meaning in their suffering and pain.[37] However, we need to be careful. Churches should be safe places in which believers are present to those in distress, yet Hauerwas reminds us there is always a danger that churches become places of isolation where people in pain

---

32. McKnight, *The Letter of James*, 133.
33. McKnight, *The Letter of James*, 132.
34. Burke, "Romans," 139.
35. Burke, "Romans," 144.
36. Menzies, *Bible Doctrines: A Pentecostal Perspective*, 148–49.
37. Swinton, "Healing Presence," 68–69.

struggle, and where there is no healing. Our hospitals may occasionally act like this because our society puts people in hospitals and sometimes forgets about them. Before long, visits from friends and the community dry up, and patients become former friends and former community members. It is a case of out-of-sight, out-of-mind. Even then, Hauerwas argues that hospitals, in many cases, are constant reminders of humanity's finiteness, as well as a sign that the community does not abandon the ill.[38] Church communities must never abandon the sick. No matter its operating income or resource pull, every church community can ease pain and has the tools to heal. The church has a rich tradition of healing and wholeness. At its fingertips, the church has everything to help people reach a healthier state of wellbeing, including the recovery from illness, trauma, or disease, all of which encompass both a natural and spiritual dynamic, including relationship restoration within society.

---

38. Hauerwas, *Suffering Presence*, 82.

9

Depression: Round Two

THE DEPRESSION RETURNED. DESPERATE, I did not know what to do. I prayed, fasted, read my Bible, and volunteered even more at church. The latter fitted in with my church's rhetoric of Christian service being the answer for everything. Even then, nothing seemed to work to stop the waves of depression, as they came and went of their own accord. Something would have to give, because each time the depression returned, it returned stronger and more intensely. I envisioned myself sitting alone in a dark room with a pack of cigarettes, a bottle of vodka, and a razor. There was no way that I would let that happen. But if the things I knew to do would not work, then what would?

Could I go back to my doctor? It had been about seven years since I saw him last. He would probably remember me because we saw each other often, and it was he whom I told Jesus had healed me from depression. What would he think if I went back and told him I was suffering from depression again? It would not say much for Jesus' healing power. I could go to another doctor, but what would be the outcome of that? After a twenty-minute talk, all my doctor would do was medicate me. How would returning to the same situation from which God delivered me bring glory to him? I could see no place in the Bible where those whom Jesus healed and delivered returned, needing healing and deliverance from the same thing again. Instead, Jesus' words to the man by the Pool of Bethesda came to mind, "Sin no more, lest a worse thing come upon you" (John 5:14). Therefore, if I was slipping back into a pattern from which God delivered me, then the responsibility for recovery was in some way on me and not on him. Nevertheless, what was I to do beyond the things that I was already doing?

THE BEGINNING OF MY SOLUTION

Things were getting worse week by week, and I felt helpless to stop it. I prayed, fasted, served at church, and performed acts of Christian service. Nothing worked, but I believe that, specifically, the acts of fasting and praying helped show me the root cause of my depression and how to handle it. In the Book of Daniel chapter 10, Daniel began praying and fasting for Israel. He wanted to understand the times and seasons for the Israelite exile in Babylon, as well as to know his people's future. Three weeks later, an angel appeared to him and explained those things for which Daniel was seeking answers. Beyond this, the angel explained why it took so long for him to arrive with the answers. He did not arrive sooner because there was a war in the spiritual realm that he needed to fight his way through with the help of the Archangel Michael. The angel said to Daniel:

> Do not fear, Daniel, for from the first day that you set your heart to understand, and to humble yourself before your God, your words were heard; and I have come because of your words. But the prince of the kingdom of Persia withstood me twenty-one days; and behold, Michael, one of the chief princes, came to help me, for I had been left alone there with the kings of Persia. Now I have come to make you understand what will happen to your people in the latter days, for the vision refers to many days yet to come.
>
> (Dan 10:12–14)

I believe that this happened to me. Prayer and fasting could not fix my depression, but they set in motion in the spiritual realm the solution to my problem, which the Lord showed to me one day during my Bible reading. Isaiah 61:3 is part of a more significant passage that describes the many acts that Jesus the Messiah would do when he came. One of these acts was to give to those who mourn "the garment of praise for the spirit of heaviness."

Looking back now, I realize that I was interpreting my situation through a Pentecostal hermeneutic. "Hermeneutic" is a term used to describe a specific way of interpreting the Bible or other texts. Different Christian traditions and schools of thought have their unique ways of interpreting the Bible and understanding it. Alan Anderson describes a Pentecostal hermeneutic as one used by those who take seriously the

Depression: Round Two

experience of the Holy Spirit in their lives as they interact with the Bible. This hermeneutic considers the interaction among the Bible, the Spirit, and the interpreter's experience in the role of fulfilling their current need. Instead of a completely literal reading of the Bible, this approach reads the Bible experientially, believing in the immediacy of the Holy Spirit who illuminates the Bible and the spiritual experiences that the Bible describes are not separate from the interpreter's own experience.[1] As Anderson says, the question with which many Pentecostals approach the Bible is, "How does this passage or verse relate to my present experience?" Within this hermeneutic, the Bible acts as "the sourcebook of miraculous answers to human need and confirmation of the reality of 'supernatural' experience."[2] It is a very distinctive hermeneutic by which one takes seriously the Holy Spirit's role in human experience for interpreting and understanding the Bible.

I did not know this hermeneutic existed back then. I just did what my instincts told me to do. I am sure many of us have approached the Bible in the same way, not knowing that what we were doing was a defined practice with its own technical term. I just did what I knew to do, and that was to prayerfully read the Bible while asking the Spirit to help me understand what I was experiencing and what to do. Because I was desperate, I also fasted much. I understood fasting as a biblical practice and discipline that Christians should regularly perform (Matt 6:16–18) and use as a tool for breakthrough (Matt 4:1–11; Acts 10:30). Like Daniel, by praying and fasting, I received the solution to my problem.

A SPIRIT OF HEAVINESS

Isaiah 61:3 reads, "The garment of praise for the spirit of heaviness." This one line is part of a broader passage of prophecy (vv. 1–3) that describes the Messiah's role. The full passage reads:

> The Spirit of the Lord God is upon Me,
> Because the Lord has anointed Me
> To preach good tidings to the poor;
> He has sent Me to heal the brokenhearted,
> To proclaim liberty to the captives,
> And the opening of the prison to those who are bound;
> To proclaim the acceptable year of the Lord,

---

1. Anderson, *Introduction to Pentecostalism*, 222–27.
2. Anderson, *Introduction to Pentecostalism*, 224.

> And the day of vengeance of our God;
> To comfort all who mourn,
> To console those who mourn in Zion,
> To give them beauty for ashes,
> The oil of joy for mourning,
> The garment of praise for the spirit of heaviness;
> That they may be called trees of righteousness,
> The planting of the Lord, that He may be glorified.

In Luke 4:16–30, Jesus applied Isaiah 61:1–2 to himself when he began his preaching ministry in Nazareth, saying, "Today this Scripture is fulfilled in your hearing." In doing this, Jesus announced himself as the fulfiller of Isaiah 61 while describing his Messianic mission. Andrew M. Davis remarks how Jesus' reading of Isaiah 61:1–2 in Nazareth makes his job as an Isaiah commentator easier, because it shows that one of the primary aims of the Book of Isaiah is to proclaim Jesus as the Messiah. Some interpreters argue that using Jesus' proclamation in Nazareth as an interpretive key for Isaiah is poor scholarship. However, Davis counters these claims by suggesting that it is unbelief for Christians to think the Holy Spirit cannot equally inspire both Isaiah 61 and Luke 4.[3]

One of the essential elements in Isaiah 61 is the fact that Jesus' role was to preach the Good News of deliverance to those who are overwhelmed, destitute, and suffering. Jesus' mission to preach came with a Holy Spirit anointing that gave him the power to do good and to heal "all" whom the devil oppressed (Acts 10:38). We see Jesus' Spirit-infused ministry releasing people from Satan's captivity throughout the Gospels. For example, Satan's captivity of one woman caused her bad back. Jesus set her free and healed her during the service in a synagogue (Luke 13:16). Likewise, Jesus also set free the man with the unclean spirit (Mark 1:23–25). Many other Gospel examples together show how Jesus' fulfillment of Isaiah 61:1–3 signified "the opening of a worldwide era of grace from almighty God, in which the debts of sin can be canceled and prisoners can be set free to worship God in joyful liberation."[4]

Within the broader passage of Isaiah 61, I saw how Jesus came to give me beauty, the oil of joy, and the garment of praise. However, I experienced none of these things. Instead, I experienced ashes, mourning, and heaviness. Still, the verse said that Jesus gave me beauty for ashes, the oil of joy

---

3. Davis, *Exalting Jesus in Isaiah*, 362.
4. Davis, *Exalting Jesus in Isaiah*, 361–63.

instead of mourning, and a garment of praise in place of heaviness. So why did I not experience these positive things? Why were the negative things submerging me? I used to experience those positive things. Something(s) that I could not account for must have happened along the way and sucked the positive things from me. Despite living my life as a Christian and trying to obey God, somehow I had lost the joy of my salvation, and instead, I was experiencing the "spirit of heaviness."

Describing depression as a "spirit of heaviness" was not outside of my understanding, especially when I considered the spiritual language that depression sufferers use to express their experiences. Swinton noted this too:.

> As one reflects upon the nature of depression it becomes clear that it is a profoundly spiritual experience that cannot be understood and dealt with through drugs and therapy alone. Its central features of profound hopelessness, loss of meaning in life, perceived loss of relationship with God or higher power, low self-esteem and general sense of purposelessness, all indicate a level of spiritual distress.[5]

Coming from a Pentecostal background, I did not see the term "spirit of heaviness" as just a simile or a metaphor for depression. I saw the "spirit of heaviness" as a literal term describing a spirit or presence typified by the experience of "heaviness." I saw a spirit or group of spirits who had a specific task to make "heavy" the hearts of humans. Additionally, I saw this second bout of depression coinciding with what Jesus said in Luke 11:24–26:

> When an unclean spirit goes out of a man, he goes through dry places, seeking rest; and finding none, he says, "I will return to my house from which I came." And when he comes, he finds it swept and put in order. Then he goes and takes with him seven other spirits more wicked than himself, and they enter and dwell there; and the last state of that man is worse than the first.

When I first received Jesus as my savior years before, he cleansed me from those spiritual influences that had dominion over my life, and he healed me. Now, though, the "spirit of heaviness" was back knocking on the door, trying to gain entry to my life. It was succeeding.

This may be a wild idea to our modern ears, but it is not so strange when we consider church history's emphasis on the role of spirits in the lives of humans, and the fact that Christians in the past believed that spirits

---

5. Swinton, *Spirituality and Mental Health Care*, 95–96.

caused depression. Furthermore, as Pentecostalism developed in the twentieth century, a resurgence took place in the belief that the spiritual realm can influence the physical realm.

Wonsuk and Julie Ma explain that our western worldview collapses the world of demons, angels, and miracles into a two-tier worldview where the natural exists on one plane and the supernatural on the other plane. They say this caused a "split-level" system where western Christians have no room in their beliefs and practices for the supernatural.[6] However, when Pentecostalism came along at the beginning of the twentieth century, its strong emphasis on miracles and healing meant that it took seriously the supernatural realm's existence.[7] From early in its history, Pentecostalism held a close relationship among Spirit-empowerment (Acts 1:8), the inevitability of Christ's return (1 Thess 4:16), and the Great Commission (Matt 28:19–20).[8] Early Pentecostals believed that they were experiencing God's manifested presence and power in the world.[9] Tongues and prophecy played essential roles, because they were the gifts through which God revealed himself and enabled those who received them to take part in the eschatological Kingdom.[10] Pentecostals believed the "Spirit's empowerment signaled a call and empowerment to be part of Jesus Christ's ongoing ministry by the power of the Spirit across cultural and geographical boundaries."[11] Pentecostalism rejected the secular/sacred dichotomy, which Ma and Ma call a two-tier worldview, and replaced it with the immediate availability of God's power, thus introducing a new reality.[12] This new reality emphasizes God's presence and power in the world.[13] This is one of the foremost reasons that Pentecostalism is growing in non-western regions.

Africa, for example, is a continent widely untouched by the west's worldview. African culture still believes that evil spirits and malevolent powers exist. They believe in the power of exorcism and divine healing, as well as the power of specialized people to invoke cursing or cures.[14] Af-

---

6. Ma and Ma, *Mission in the Spirit*, 181.
7. Ma and Ma, *Mission in the Spirit*, 184.
8. Klaus, "The Holy Spirit and Mission," 328.
9. Dobson, "Gifted for Change," 52.
10. Dobson, "Gifted for Change," 57.
11. Klaus, "The Holy Spirit and Mission," 324–25.
12. Klaus, "The Holy Spirit and Mission," 324–25.
13. Dobson, "Gifted for Change," 52.
14. Asamoah-Gyadu, "Pulling down Strongholds," 308, citing Brigit Meyer, *Translating*

rican culture operates within a different worldview from the west because it has followed a different cultural and intellectual path.[15] The same is true of Indian culture.[16] They do not have to be convinced that the spiritual realm exists, as many westerners do, because they are already aware of its existence. In such cultures, Pentecostalism's emphasis on the Holy Spirit's supernatural role is an innovative and practical approach to evangelizing a culture focused on the supernatural. Pentecostalism's consistency with the culture's traditional religious ideas is more consistent with a biblical cosmology, which sees no distinction between the supernatural and the natural.[17]

When I considered my earlier experience of depression and the ineffectiveness of the antidepressants, I realized they were ineffective because they sought to fix the chemical imbalance in my brain that caused my depression. Unfortunately, though, they could not fix the spiritual root causing the chemical imbalance. What I am saying is that the influence of the spiritual, as it operates as part of God's creation, affected me physically. Luke 13:10–17 is one scriptural example that springs to mind:

> Now He was teaching in one of the synagogues on the Sabbath. And behold, there was a woman who had a spirit of infirmity eighteen years, and was bent over and could in no way raise herself up. But when Jesus saw her, He called her to Him and said to her, "Woman, you are loosed from your infirmity." And He laid His hands on her, and immediately she was made straight, and glorified God.
>
> But the ruler of the synagogue answered with indignation, because Jesus had healed on the Sabbath; and he said to the crowd, "There are six days on which men ought to work; therefore come and be healed on them, and not on the Sabbath day."

---

the Devil: Religion and Modernity Among the Ewe in Ghana (Edinburgh, UK: Edinburgh University Press, 1999), xiii.

15. Asamoah-Gyadu, "Pulling down Strongholds," 310–11, citing Kwame Bediako, "Worship as Vital Participation: Some Personal Reflections on Ministry in the African Church," *Journal of African Christian Thought* 8 (December 2005) 3.

16. Michael Bergunder, "Miracle healing and exorcism," 111. In his study of Pentecostalism in India, Bergunder observed how Pentecostalism interacted with the traditional religious beliefs. He noted that the experience of the Holy Spirit's supernatural power established a robust phenomenological connection with conventional Indian religion.

17. Thisleton, *A Shorter Guide to the Holy Spirit*, 39.

> The Lord then answered him and said, "Hypocrite! Does not each one of you on the Sabbath loose his ox or donkey from the stall, and lead it away to water it? So ought not this woman, being a daughter of Abraham, whom Satan has bound—think of it—for eighteen years, be loosed from this bond on the Sabbath?" And when He said these things, all His adversaries were put to shame; and all the multitude rejoiced for all the glorious things that were done by Him.

Notice that this took place inside the synagogue. To put it in a present-day context: she was a church attendee who suffered from a bad back caused by Satan. It is clear from the passage that something troubled her in the spiritual realm that manifested in the physical realm—just like my depression. So, when Jesus set her free, he dealt with the spiritual root of the problem that had a physical consequence.

I am not saying demons possessed me and caused my depression, and I do not want to open up a discussion on demonology. However, when we consider what we discussed in chapter 3 about the role of demons in causing mental illness, strong biblical evidence exists for spiritual influences causing somatic abnormalities in the physical. This is not to say that we should forget the role our physical and psychological environment might also play in this interaction.

PUTTING ON THE GARMENT OF PRAISE

One line from Isaiah 61:3, "The garment of praise for the spirit of heaviness," told me what I was dealing with had a spiritual source. Right away, I saw a sharp contrast between the garment of praise and the spirit of heaviness. The image came to mind of taking off one garment drenched in misery and despair and replacing it with a garment that was light and jubilant. I knew what I had to do if I wanted to get rid of this spirit of heaviness—I had to put on the garment of praise. I had to praise the Lord.

Around the time when I saw this truth from Isaiah 61:3, I realized that two of the fundamental features of depression are how it causes hopelessness and loss of life's meaning. Swinton says that if a person's life has no hope, then it has no meaning; and if a person's life has no hope, then the person will die either physically or emotionally.[18] The Epistle to the Hebrews links faith with hope. Hebrews 11:1 says, "Now faith is the

---

18. Swinton, *Spirituality and Mental Health Care*, 112.

substance of things hoped for, the evidence of things not seen." Chapter 11 in Hebrews shows in significant detail how faithful people lived throughout biblical history, enduring and overcoming many difficulties because they lived by faith, having hope in God's future kingdom (Heb 11:13–16). In other words, they had hope because their lives had purpose. They might not have had a full revelation of the purpose for which they lived, hence their need to have faith, but they still had hope and purpose. This is why depression is so lethal: it erodes the sufferer's hope. And in doing so, depression can destroy their purpose and undermine their faith.

Although depression causes this lethal problem, the Bible explains how to fight back. As I was still meditating on what the Lord showed me through Isaiah 61:3, I began reading the Psalms. Something in Psalm 42:5 spoke to me, "Why are you cast down, O my soul, and why are you in turmoil within me? Hope in God; for I shall again praise him, my salvation" (ESV). I realized what I had to do to combat depression's lethal onslaught: I had to build up my hope. And Psalm 42:5 told me how: I had to speak to my soul. I admire the way that Charles Spurgeon describes this psalm:

> It is the cry of a man far removed from the outward ordinances and worship of God, sighing for the long loved house of his God; and at the same time it is the voice of a spiritual believer, under depressions, longing for the renewal of the divine presence, struggling with doubts and fears, but yet holding his ground by faith in the living God. But rather than succumbing to it, he speaks to his soul and commands it to praise the Lord.[19]

Genesis 2:7 (KJV) says, "And the LORD God formed man of the dust of the ground, and breathed into his nostrils the breath of life; and man became a living soul." J. P. Moreland explains that the soul is the essence that makes the body a human body in that it "diffuses, informs, animates, develops, unifies and grounds the biological functions of its body."[20] The Hebrew word for soul is *nephesh*, which Ashbrook says refers to the principle of human life. He observes that as living souls, the Bible sees humans as a composite of two factors: fleshly parts and the soul. These both mix to form the human body.[21] The ancient Hebrews believed there was such a close relationship between the flesh and the soul that the soul was resident

---

19. Spurgeon, "Psalm 42."
20. Moreland and Rae, *Body and Soul*, 202.
21. Ashbrook, "The Functional Meaning of the Soul," 3.

in the blood.²² As biblical ontology developed, *ruach* emerged as the relational aspect through which humans commune with God. *Ruach* has many meanings in the Bible (e.g., breath, wind, spirit, etc.), but so far as it relates to a person's relationship with God, scholars often translate it as "spirit." Therefore, the human spirit is distinguishable from the soul and body, but it is not separate from them.²³ Simply put, *nephesh* makes humans live, and *ruach* allows them to relate with God.

We see, right away, that the biblical idea of humanity is that of unity. The Bible describes us as a singular entity rooted in a physical body.²⁴ Yet, this does not mean that our soul and spirit do not have any measurable properties. The attributes of the soul and spirit are visible through our thoughts, actions, and emotional responses.²⁵ Since our soul animates us, makes us alive, is a part of our being, and to some extent our fleshly body is the outward form of the soul,²⁶ we should not think it remarkable that we can speak to and encourage our soul.

This is what I did. When the feelings of fear, anxiety, and hopelessness tried to come over me, I spoke to my soul. I told it to praise the Lord, and I forced myself to do so (Ps 42:11; 146:1). It was the hardest thing in the world to do, because hopelessness and despair so overpowered my emotions that I just wanted to submit and wallow in the mud. But I persevered. No way would I ever return to that lonely apartment room with a bottle of vodka and antidepressants as my friends while cutting myself with a razor.

With the bit between my teeth, I went alone into our spare room and began singing church songs. When my memory ran dry, or I got bored—which was more often than not—I started offering the Lord praise and thanksgiving. I said things like, "God, I love you and praise you. I magnify your holy name." During these times, sometimes I broke off into prayer and thanked him for deliverance, or I spoke in tongues. I did not know it then, but as I practiced these activities of praise and worship, I engaged in the process of worship and liturgy that Swinton says helps depression sufferers at an experiential level.²⁷ He explains that although sufferers might not fully comprehend their feelings, healing power still flows through the expressive

---

22. Niebuhr, *The Nature and Destiny of Man*, 13.
23. Ashbrook, "The Functional Meaning of the Soul," 4.
24. Weaver, "Senile Dementia and a Resurrection Theology," 446.
25. Moreland and Rae, *Body and Soul*, 200.
26. Ashbrook, "The Functional Meaning of the Soul," 3.
27. Swinton, *Spirituality and Mental Health Care*, 125.

outlet of worship, enabling sufferers to process experientially what their intellect cannot.[28]

As I did these things, the Lord showed me the richness of the Psalms, which was the songbook of the Old Testament saints and the early church. I took a childlike view and concluded:

> Humans write praise and worship songs about God, sometimes with the aid of the Holy Spirit. However, since the Psalms are in the Bible, and God wrote the Bible, then the Psalms are the praise and worship songs that God wrote about himself for our benefit.

I took this idea to heart and read the Psalms aloud. Before beginning, I said something like, "Lord, I am reciting the Psalms as praise and thanksgiving to you. Let their expression of praise, thanksgiving, and worship be an outlet for mine. May their expressions of prayer, supplication, and frustrations be an avenue for mine. I praise you through the words of the psalmist." Then I began reading each psalm aloud, one after another. It was very challenging, but I read the Psalms until the feelings of hopelessness and despair lifted. Sometimes this took minutes, and sometimes hours. Honestly, it was boring, but there was no way I was going back to medication, alcohol, and razors. So, I read, and I read, and I read again.

Over the weeks and months, the hours of boredom paid off, and the depression slowly went away. Peace, joy, and the hope that the Lord was my strength, replaced the feelings of depression. Whenever I saw the darkness rising, I marched into the spare room with my Bible under my arm and praised the Lord until my throat was dry. The depression subsided so gradually that I never noticed it subsiding at all. Then one day, the depression left, and it has never come back.

---

28. Swinton, *Spirituality and Mental Health Care*, 139.

10

Fighting Depression Using the Psalms

ALONE IN MY SPARE room, I sang Christian songs, spoke in tongues, and offered praise and thanksgiving to God. When my memory ran dry, or I got bored, I read the Psalms aloud one after another, and I read them for as long as my schedule allowed, or until the feelings of depression went away and my spirit lightened. I did not know it then, but each time I marched into our spare bedroom with my Bible in hand and praised the Lord and recited the Psalms, I was engaging in a broader Christian tradition. This is a tradition which, Swinton says, helps sufferers because it allows them to identify with the images and feelings that are portrayed in the Psalms, thus providing a template for them to make sense of their own experiences.[1] Although I never read Swinton's study until years later, what he describes compares with my healing and deliverance from depression. I see now that God led me to use the Scriptures, specifically the Psalms, to heal me.

THE PSALMS AND QUESTIONS OF "WHY ME?"

The natural reaction of many people when they experience depression, or any complaint that causes suffering, is to ask profound questions about God's role in their lives. "Why did God let this happen?" "If God is good, then why do terrible things happen?" We all know these types of questions, because we have all asked them at some point in our lives. These are questions of theodicy, and they are all variations of the principal question, "How

---
1. Swinton, *Spirituality and Mental Health Care*, 130.

could a God of power and love allow this to happen to me?"[2] According to Simon Dein and others, asking such questions is a positive thing. By asking them, sufferers enter a process through which their search for answers provides meaning and significance to the events that caused their suffering. In the interaction, Christians search for an explanation into the role of evil and God in their lives. Their search has the potential to help them hold on to their understanding of a loving and perfectly good God who still has a plan for their lives despite their suffering. Through these processes, sufferers reorientate themselves physically and spiritually amid everything that is happening around them, the result of which can be positive or negative. A positive outcome results in sufferers turning to religion for support that leads towards positive mental health outcomes. A negative result causes a religious struggle that is typified by doubt and poor social functioning.[3]

Sometimes, though, it is possible that people experiencing suffering might ask questions of anthropodicy instead of theodicy. Questions of anthropodicy do not have God as the questioner's subject. Instead, anthropodicy questions are based on the questioner's lifestyle, and seek to justify humanity as good. Within this dynamic, questions of pain and suffering usually surface with questions like, "What did I do to deserve this? Was it my diet? My lack of exercise?" Generally, anthropodicy questions are structured around what the sufferers themselves did or did not do to cause their distress. As usefully reflective as such questions appear, the sufferer's intention in asking them is usually to justify themselves in light of their suffering. Either way, the outcome of the sufferer's questioning process involves the believer's God-image and God-concept. "God-concept" is a term used to describe what one believes about God. It contrasts with the "God-image," which is a term used to describe a person's emotional or relational experience of God. Consistency between the two brings healing. Unresolved discrepancies between them or negative experiences of God can complicate the healing and growth processes.[4]

Properly tackled, theodicy questions can provide those suffering from depression with an explanatory framework through which they can interpret their experiences and arrive at a greater understanding of God's character.[5] This, in turn, provides a particular redemptive aspect to their

---

2. Dein et al., "Theodicy and End-of-Life Care," 194–95
3. Dein et al., "Theodicy and End-of-Life Care," 193–95.
4. Dein et al., "Theodicy and End-of-Life Care," 205.
5. Dein et al., "Theodicy and End-of-Life Care," 191.

suffering that positively affects their wellbeing. I believe that the Psalms provide the perfect medium to explore theodicy questions because they help sufferers find meaning and hope. An essential element in this process is the role the Psalms play in assisting sufferers to express their feelings during those times when their intellect cannot comprehend what they are experiencing. Speaking about one of his research participants, Swinton says, "When she did not have words to express her agony, she allows these simple words to become a vehicle for the expression of her psychological pain and the deep spiritual need."[6]

Using the Bible to combat depression, especially using the Book of Psalms, is meaningful to me. I used the Psalms as an outlet to communicate what I was experiencing. This allowed me to reflect on my experiences while considering the psalmist's experiences. Swinton mentions this phenomenon and explains that because this approach is not cognitive, sufferers can break through the intellectual barriers that typify depression. The participant travels with the psalmist through the turmoil to a place of renewed faith and trust in God. "In this way, the Bible provides the language that formulates the boundaries within which one understands and expresses their experiences of depression."[7] Pauline Nelson makes a very astute observation, "The psalmist did not ask to escape the valley of the shadow of death, only to have God walk through it with him."[8] This relational reading of the scriptures provides those struggling with depression with the certainty that God is with them throughout their experiences.

THE PSALMS OF LAMENT

The Old Testament scholar Walter Brueggemann says that the Psalms are Israel's primal utterances of affirmation and distress to God, and that they have proven themselves as timeless and universal guides to worship and faith for both Jews and Christians.[9] The Psalms do not seek to explain life; rather, they offer a picture of life's reality that includes the full spectrum of human emotions, from our happiest moments to our most soul-destroying moments. As Logan Jones says, "The words of the Psalms speak to the

---

6. Swinton, *Spirituality and Mental Health Care*, 129.
7. Swinton, *Spirituality and Mental Health Care*, 130–31.
8. Nelson, "My Father's Hands," 82.
9. Brueggemann, *An Introduction to the Old Testament*, 277.

very core of the human experience."[10] Our western culture boasts of being transparent and of "keeping things real," but the emotions expressed in the Psalms are more real and open than most of us are comfortable, never mind writing them in a book for others to read. The psalmist, though, did not hesitate. He gave full voice to God of the things he felt and experienced, whether fear, anger, frustration, or doubt.

In the practice of many contemporary churches, though, Brueggemann believes that we have lost such negative expressions. He states that the church's propensity has been to deny this process, assuming such expressions are negative and are akin to disobedience and unfaithfulness to God. Because of this, Brueggemann argues, the church has lost the essential human ability to lament.[11] Bruce Waltke and his colleagues believe that our modern churches do not practice lament because contemporary society is unwilling to face the fact of our absolute need. Many people among us suffer because we are reluctant to express ourselves truthfully to God and to express our pain.[12] Jones reminds us, though, that if our relationship with God is authentic, then we need not worry about respectability, because honest dialogue and truthful expression make genuine relationships thrive. Silence only leads to pain, but lament breaks the silence and leads to wholeness. As Jones says, "The anguish of life calls for speech, for words, for prayer."[13] Since prayer is communion with God, the Psalms get down and dirty into the pit of human life and teach us how to communicate with God in a way that holds nothing back. We present our hopes, dreams, and praise to God, as well as our fears, pain, and unbelief. The Psalms teach us how to stand faithfully before God as we wait on him to act, seek answers, and hope beyond hope. The Psalms are "human life and action, teaching us how to stand faithfully in life and prayer."[14]

That over one-third of the Psalms are lament psalms establishes the importance of lament as a human function.[15] It shows that experiencing anguish and confusion in life is not a sign that our faith is deficient or that we lack faith. When life careens out of control, and negative feelings and

---

10. Jones, "The Psalms of Lament," 47.
11. Brueggemann, *An Introduction to the Old Testament*, 289.
12. Waltke et al., *The Psalms As Christian Lament*, 3–4.
13. Jones, "The Psalms of Lament," 49.
14. Jones, "The Psalms of Lament," 47.
15. Waltke et al., *The Psalms As Christian Lament*, 1; Brueggemann, *An Introduction to the Old Testament*, 289.

questions emerge, then these negative feelings are not necessarily cues that we need to "grow up" and have more faith. In fact, these experiences of puzzlement and anguish are "intrinsic to the very nature of our faith."[16] The bodily postures that the Psalms convey ought to convince us of this. They describe outstretched arms, kneeling in supplication, or lying abandoned in the dirt. The Psalms' language of pouring out the body and spirit in times of grief expresses raw, barren human emotion. Waltke et al. write, "Lament and confession as expressed in the psalms both require that one stand in the presence of God as Sovereign and Holy Lord, implying accountability, openness to the Other, awareness of sin, of personal shortcoming, and of attribution of the whole cosmos to the Creator."[17]

Our lives are one giant transition from birth to death, between which we have many good and bad experiences, but then we have the ultimate experience when we meet Jesus in person. Jones explains how the focus of much of today's preaching and theology is often on this happy ending and the fact that everything will eventually be hunky-dory. Jones criticizes this approach because it does not consider the events that happen during life's sojourn. Joy may be God's final word on the matter, but until we get there, life's pilgrimage sometimes takes unexpected turns where angst and puzzlement abound. During these difficult times, lament may express much of our earthly sojourn.[18]

Biblical lament fits into a pattern of transition through which the sufferer moves from pain and fear towards faith. Brueggemann uses the language of "plea-to-praise" to describe this transition.[19] Jones mentions how the transition is essential to understanding the lament psalms:

> The reality of brokenness and grief is not denied in the laments. But—and this "but" is a critical aspect of the movement—the movement does not stay stuck in the plea, in brokenness and grief. There is more beyond. There is ultimately praise. There is an unparalleled transformation of sorrow into something more, call it praise, joy, wisdom, joy, hope.[20]

---

16. Waltke et al., *The Psalms As Christian Lament*, 1, citing R. W. L. Moberly, "Lament," *New International Dictionary of Old Testament Theology & Exegesis*, IV, 879.
17. Waltke et al., *The Psalms As Christian Lament*, 2.
18. Jones, "The Psalms of Lament," 48.
19. Brueggemann, *An Introduction to the Old Testament*, 282.
20. Jones, "The Psalms of Lament," 48.

Within this transition from plea-to-praise, the Psalms do not dismiss, deny, or seek to avoid sorrow and suffering. Instead, the Psalms give meaning during times of grief that transform pain into faith, peace, and joy in the Lord. The Psalms allow us to progress through the darkness of the valley of the shadow of death, knowing that God is with us in our suffering. Lament witnesses to a profound faith in God and deepens our relationship with the Lord as we faithfully join him in an honest dialogue about our lives.[21]

FROM PLEA TO PRAISE: CRY-HEAR-THANK

Brueggemann describes different types of psalms and their structures, but of particular importance to us are the psalms of lament. These are a genre of speech that an individual or group uses to express personal distress to God. Using Psalm 13, Brueggemann summarizes the typical lament structure in this psalm genre.[22]

The speaker begins with a complaint:

> How long, O Lord? Will You forget me forever?
> How long will You hide Your face from me?
> How long shall I take counsel in my soul,
> Having sorrow in my heart daily?
> How long will my enemy be exalted over me?
> (vv. 1–2)

The petition follows next:

> Consider and hear me, O Lord my God;
> Enlighten my eyes.
> (v. 3a)

Then the psalmist gives reasons for the Lord to intervene:

> Lest I sleep the sleep of death;
> Lest my enemy say,
> "I have prevailed against him";
> Lest those who trouble me rejoice when I am moved.
> (vv. 3b–4)

Finally, the psalmist comes to some kind of resolution about everything that he is experiencing, and he promises praise to God:

---

21. Jones, "The Psalms of Lament," 49.
22. Brueggemann, *An Introduction to the Old Testament*, 281–82.

> But I have trusted in Your mercy;
> My heart shall rejoice in Your salvation.
> I will sing to the Lord,
> Because He has dealt bountifully with me.
> (vv. 5–6)

Throughout this psalm, a dramatic interactive moment occurs in which the psalmist's lament forms an ordered interaction of "cry-hear-thank."[23] This is a fluid process of conceptualizing and understanding the psalmist's feelings within a framework that sees all of his positive and negative expressions taking place within a life of faith.

Jones explains how Brueggemann's scheme provides us with a way of seeing the whole of the Psalms as foundational to the life of faith, revealing that they are entirely in touch with everything that goes on in our lives, including all the bad and all the good. Jones recognizes that some psalms express anguish and frustration in ways that may seem opposed to a life of faith. Although these expressions may seem harmful, he affirms that they still facilitate the move into a deeper transformative faith.[24] This move into a deeper transformative faith occurs as the psalmist goes through a decisive three-stage process from orientation to disorientation, and then to a new-orientation.[25]

According to Brueggemann, orientation is when everything is going along fine as usual; it is when we are uneventfully getting on and enjoying our lives with nothing rattling the status quo. Our family is healthy, our job is secure, and the car has no engine warning lights coming on. When we are at a place of orientation, our lives go along as usual, and everything happens as expected. Disorientation occurs when something out of the ordinary or terrible happens. This could be job loss, death, ill health, or something like that. Some form of awakening takes place through which we question aspects of life or doubt some things about our belief system. So far as this transition from orientation to disorientation occurs in the Psalms, the psalmist's move from security to insecurity causes deep emotional responses. Jones provides a hypothetical example:

> The call comes into the Pastoral Care office late one afternoon. The nurse says, "Chaplain, would you please come see Mr. Smith in 5080? He has just gotten some bad news and . . ." Her voice

---

23. Brueggemann, *An Introduction to the Old Testament*, 284
24. Jones, "The Psalms of Lament," 49–50.
25. Brueggemann, *An Introduction to the Old Testament*, 288.

trails off. The rest of this nurse's referral is left unsaid. It turns out Mr. Smith, a 45-year old married man with two teenage daughters, has learned he has pancreatic cancer. The doctors say he has about three or four months to live, six at the most. Upon arrival on the unit, the nurse tells the chaplain that Mr. Smith is "upset." She suggests that a pastoral visit from the chaplain would make him "feel better." In other words, if Mr. Smith "feels better," then he will be an easier patient for which to care. How the chaplain responds to this referral depends, in part, on his or her theological understanding of the psalms of lament and the process of orientation—disorientation—new orientation.[26]

I quoted Jones extensively to show the motivation behind the doctor's appeal for the chaplain to intervene. The motivation being, that if Mr. Jones feels better, the doctor will find it easier to interact with him. I wanted to emphasize this point because prescribing medication is not the only way to make life easier. Sometimes the intervention of other professionals helps too. In this sense, the doctor is looking to satiate Mr. Smith's suffering by the quickest means, which fits our culture's therapeutic approach to life. Similarly, when faced with the suffering that is caused by depression, it is all too easy to adopt our Christian culture's prominent strategy of positive confession and say a quick prayer asking for comfort, to claim healing, or to rebuke the demon of depression. Those simple acts, though, which might be considered therapeutic, may hinder the sufferer from moving from disorientation to a new-orientation, because these acts stop the sufferer from doing what he or she needs to do in order to receive healing—those hurting do not need our advice, they need to know that it is okay to lament sometimes.

Mr. Smith's unexpected diagnosis has jolted him from orientation to disorientation. As with any move in this manner, there is no simple solution. Using the Psalms for lament is a long, arduous process. It is a process in which Mr. Smith may have to get worse before he gets better. Jones explains, "What Mr. Smith needs in this time of trial, I believe, is a lament. He needs to be able to cry out to God, to complain about the unfairness of this diagnosis and the fact he will not see his teenagers graduate from college. He needs to make his appeal to God."[27] The lament psalms can help sufferers of depression in the same way they can help Mr. Smith. "The

---

26. Jones, "The Psalms of Lament," 54.
27. Jones, "The Psalms of Lament," 54–5.

psalmsndeed speak the unspeakable and name the unnamable."[28] By using the Psalms, they give those who are in pain the time, space, and permission, to own their disorientation and to process what they are experiencing, as well as what it means for themselves and their loved ones.

This idea of accepting disorientation and the feelings that it causes might go against the Christian tradition of some people. In such a case, some might argue against using the Psalms in this way, speculating that embracing pain and suffering and working through these feelings are conducive to unbelief. Instead, the solution would be to use the biblical text, select the correct scriptures, and positively confess them to increase faith and to claim healing. There is nothing wrong with this approach, but as we said, sometimes there is no quick fix. Inevitably, we go through seasons in life when pain seems to be our only companion. This is the stage where we follow the psalmist's lead and cry out in anguish and despair in ways that we might not consider Christian.

When we lament, we unleash our feelings to God. It is these wailings that reorient us and take us out of disorientation. Although the period of disorientation and lament may feel like it has lasted, and will last, forever, something happens in lament, and God responds. At this point, we begin to move from the point of disorientation toward a new orientation. The Spirit assures us that God has heard and is responding/has responded/will respond. As Jones says, "From Sheol, from the pit, new life emerges, and the response in reply to this new life is one of thanksgiving and praise."[29] Although we might not understand how the Spirit worked and how this move happened, we enter a new place of orientation in which life has stabilized. Newly orientated, we are now wiser and more alert, and we have a keener understanding of God and human life than before. We may still have questions and not totally understand what we went through, but overall we enter a new phase of life with a healthier outlook, as well as with a heart warmed to praise and thank God. No one forgets their experience of lament. At a practical level, this is so we can minister to and help others. Nevertheless, the excitement of this new life brings about praise and thanksgiving to God for his deliverance and intervention. It is characterized by a "rush of positive responses, including delight, amazement, wonder, awe, gratitude, and thanksgiving."[30]

---

28. Jones, "The Psalms of Lament," 54.
29. Jones, "The Psalms of Lament," 49–50.
30. Jones, "The Psalms of Lament," 51.

Lament is not about fixing the pain, casting it off, or denying the hopelessness. Instead, lament is about journeying with God—sometimes reluctantly or against our wishes—and him taking us from a place of disorientation to a new orientation. Where rejuvenated, we acknowledge God in praise and thanksgiving. This metaphor of journey fits in well with our discussion on healing earlier in this book, in which we described healing as the processes involved in reaching a healthier state of being. Healing is a journey towards wholeness and refers to everything that is required to recover from illness, trauma, or disease. Healing encompasses both a natural dynamic and spiritual dynamic, and it includes the restoration of relationships within society.[31] When we use lament along this journey, God turns our lament into a song of praise. We may never want to go through that experience again, nor wish it upon anyone else, but we will be thankful for the experience.

BEWARE THE BOREDOM

My reading of the Psalms was not as dramatic as this chapter implies. I believe that those authors whom I cited are correct in their observations, and that a mystery exists in the simple act of reading the Psalms, through which the Spirit somehow works to bring healing. However, my experience of reading the Psalms in my spare room was anything but dramatic. There were no flashes of lightning and rolls of thunder. I was not alone on the mountain top, caught up in the euphoria of God's glory surrounded by the multitude of the angelic choir. No, not at all. I sat cross-legged on the carpet with my Bible on my lap, bored out of my brains, and my voice parched, as I read each psalm line-by-line. The only activity in the entire room were the sounds of the pages turning and me speaking the psalmist's words, at times interspersed with praying in tongues.

I want to hammer home this point. I have had intense spiritual experiences before, but as I went through this process of psalm reading, rarely did I experience anything that I could refer to as remotely spiritual. There was no battle in which I stormed the gates of hell and won my breakthrough. Rarely did I weep at the words of the text as they penetrated my heart. Although it may be different for others, there was nothing like that for me. I say this to clarify that this process excluded my emotions, other than reading the Psalms and praising the Lord until I no longer felt depressed.

---

31. Leathard, "Healing in the Christian Tradition," 33.

Ultimately, the Spirit's healing power was at work behind the scenes, because the depression eased and went away over the weeks and months. It has never come back.

I believe reciting the Psalms worked because God gave them to us for the very reason that we might fully express ourselves within the frailty of this creation. Battling depression by using the Psalms (i.e., God's Word) worked because it is the very nature of God's Word to work (Eph 6:17; Heb 4:12). I still get sad and sometimes feel down, but as anyone who has suffered from depression knows, there is an enormous difference between experiencing depression and just having an off day. Even then, the solution is the same—praising the Lord.

11

Depression, Where is Your Sting?

THIS CHAPTER DRAWS THE book to a conclusion by discussing how asking God for help and obediently acting upon the support he provides contributes towards the broader conversation of sanctification and depression. I show how I learned obedience and grew in Christlikeness through the life experiences that contributed to my depression and how I received healing through reading the Psalms. Since the Spirit used my suffering to help others, my story acts as a paradigm demonstrating sanctification within and through the community.

ASKING FOR FREEDOM FROM DEPRESSION

In the Book of Matthew, Jesus said:

> Ask, and it will be given to you; seek, and you will find; knock, and it will be opened to you. For everyone who asks receives, and he who seeks finds, and to him who knocks it will be opened. Or what man is there among you who, if his son asks for bread, will give him a stone? Or if he asks for a fish, will he give him a serpent? If you then, being evil, know how to give good gifts to your children, how much more will your Father who is in heaven give good things to those who ask Him!
>
> (Matt 7:7–11)

In this passage, Jesus gives us permission to ask God for good things. Is it a good thing to ask God for mental health and for freedom from depression?

I think so. Third John 1:2 says, "Beloved, I pray that you may prosper in all things and be in health, just as your soul prospers." Prospering "in all things" and being "in health" correspond to the flourishing and healthiness of our souls as they experience wholeness and continue to develop wholeness through lives that are lived in relationship with God. Therefore, when we ask God for good things, there is nothing wrong with asking the Lord to help us physically and mentally experience and enjoy health and wellbeing. Indeed, it is a great privilege that God allows us to ask him for good things.

Since Jesus permits us to ask God for good things, and mental health is one of those good things, then we must have confidence that we will receive the good things that we request. First John 5:14–15 says:

> Now this is the confidence that we have in Him, that if we ask anything according to his will, He hears us. And if we know that He hears us, whatever we ask, we know that we have the petitions that we have asked of Him.

This verse basically tells us that Jesus will give us the things we ask for, if it is his will for us to have them. Since Jesus permitted us to ask for good things, and if mental health is a good thing, then we can assume that God wants to answer our request for continued wellbeing and health in that area. Asking for and receiving our requests on this matter is not so much an act of faith on our part; it has more to do with the integrity of God's character and him granting our requests as he said he would.

Despite the simplicity of asking God for help, even this simple action may be problematic for depression sufferers, because a division exists between how they feel and think about God, and this affects how they interact with him. A depression sufferer may not have it in them to ask God for help. In this event, we refer to the fact that despite depression's effects, the Spirit still unites believers in Christ's life (Col 3:3), and in him, they live and move and have their being (Acts 17:28). Even if depression strangles the believer from requesting God for help, the "Spirit also helps in our weaknesses. For we do not know what we should pray for as we ought, but the Spirit Himself makes intercession for us with groanings which cannot be uttered" (Rom 8:26).

It is remarkable to think that the Holy Spirit, acting as our counselor (John 14:26), can traverse the complexities of our minds, wills, and emotions, and can get right down deep inside each of us and formulate prayer to God on our behalf. The Spirit works behind the scenes to move us from disorientation to orientation by untangling all those things going on inside us that we find impossible to articulate. If we cannot ask God for help, then the Spirit petitions God on our behalf.

Perhaps just as remarkable is that we can participate with the Spirit in this process. We quoted Romans 8:26 above. Pentecostals regularly see this verse as a reference to praying in tongues. By praying in tongues, although our mind is unfruitful (1 Cor 14:14) and we do not know precisely what we are praying for, somehow we facilitate the above process. This is not to say that the Spirit cannot petition God on our behalf without us praying in tongues, because he can. Instead, praying in tongues is a voluntary act on our part that, among other things, allows us to demonstrate our submissiveness to the Spirit's inner working. By praying in tongues, we partner with the Spirit as he descends to the depths of our being and takes everything that is going on inside us and puts it before God. As Simon Chan describes, tongues act as a means of grace through which the Spirit draws us into greater intimacy with God, lessening our will and desires, and conforming us to God.[1] Therefore, praying in tongues is one means through which we grow in grace into the image of Christ (which is the process of sanctification). As we share in God's life and holiness through Jesus, our lives become a journey into a more in-depth understanding and experience of health. In this journey, praying in tongues serves as a useful tool to develop wholeness (i.e., *shalom*), thus strengthening us (1 Cor 14:4).

We discussed praying in tongues a little here, but I do not want to put off anyone who does not speak in tongues. As essential and useful as the gift of tongues is, and even though it is a gift to desire earnestly (1 Cor 12:31), it is not the be-all and end-all of the Christian life. As praying in tongues relates to depression, I see a link between tongues and reading the Psalms in the way that both hasten us along the journey of sanctification and help us grow in Christ's image. Like tongues, the psalmist's written words give voice to those groanings inside us that are too deep for us to formulate into words. The Spirit has used the psalmist's pen ahead of time to help us express what we are experiencing. Therefore, in the same way that tongues act as a sanctifying tool that takes our deep groanings and puts them before God, the Psalms also act as a sanctifying tool. By being a sanctifying tool, reading the Psalms moves us forward in Christlikeness and develops within us Christ's sound mind.

---

1. Chan, *Pentecostal Theology*, 81.

OBEDIENTLY ACTING UPON THE HELP THAT GOD OFFERS

I received insight as I spent time alone with God and asked him for help, but I did not know that the understanding that I received was God's answer to my cry for help. One of the significant insights I received was to use the Book of Psalms during my prayer time. As I previously said, the revelation was this: Humans write praise and worship songs about God, sometimes with the Holy Spirit's aid. However, since the Psalms are in the Bible, and God wrote the Bible, then the Psalms are the praise and worship songs that God wrote about himself for our benefit.

Looking back now, this revelation did not come out of a vacuum. My mind formed it from a mixture of sources and from many places. For instance, around the time when I experienced the second bout of depression, I heard a teaching on the Psalms that made me think about them in a new way. I also had gone through three years of theological study, years of Bible reading, book reading, prayer, and the general life experiences of living every day as a Christian. So, I cannot claim that this revelation came to me out of nowhere. Instead, the Spirit wove together threads from these sources and from many others, to present me with the insight that I needed. All God required of me was that I obey his instruction, and I did so—albeit ignorantly, because at the time, I did not know that the insight I received about the Psalms was the answer to my prayer and the solution to my problem. Remember in the Book of Daniel, how the angel came and spoke to Daniel and gave him the information he requested? Well, my angel had come and gone, leaving me with the information I needed to solve my problem, but I did not realize it. Nevertheless, I was obedient to what I knew I could do and should do.

Although society and culture may have silenced the church, our broader Christian tradition is not silent. Fantastic stories of spiritual titans and prayer warriors fill our history, people whose lives teach us what to do when we are in trouble. I remembered stories of people like William Seymour, "Praying" John Hyde, Smith Wigglesworth, John Wesley, and many others who showed unusual prayerfulness and devotion to God. Even Moses', Elijah's, and Jesus' practices of prayer and fasting motivated me. I acted on my knowledge of the lives and spiritual practices of those who had gone before me and tried to put into practice what they did. Suppose I just sat on the couch, depressed, watching TV, and thinking about asking God for healing and deliverance from depression—I doubt I would ever have won the battle.

A similar thing happened to Bartimaeus in Luke 18:35–43:

> Then it happened, as He was coming near Jericho, that a certain blind man sat by the road begging. And hearing a multitude passing by, he asked what it meant. So they told him that Jesus of Nazareth was passing by. And he cried out, saying, "Jesus, Son of David, have mercy on me!"
>
> Then those who went before warned him that he should be quiet; but he cried out all the more, "Son of David, have mercy on me!"
>
> So Jesus stood still and commanded him to be brought to Him. And when he had come near, He asked him, saying, "What do you want Me to do for you?"
>
> He said, "Lord, that I may receive my sight."
>
> Then Jesus said to him, "Receive your sight; your faith has made you well." And immediately he received his sight, and followed Him, glorifying God. And all the people, when they saw it, gave praise to God.

The fact blind Bartimaeus called out shows that he knew of Jesus. Bartimaeus' knowledge may have come from one of those who spread the news (Matt 4:14; 8:32–34; Mark 1:27–28; Luke 4:36–37) or one of Jesus' missionaries (Luke 10). Even then, although he had heard about Jesus and knew that he was passing by, Bartimaeus could easily have sat quietly and held his peace amid the peer pressure. He may have thought, "What if Jesus does not help me?" or "How will disobeying my community affect their giving?" Despite these fears, and although those closest to him tried to silence him, Bartimaeus had to be true to what he knew to do. He could not sit begging anymore, so he did what he knew to do and called out, and by calling out, Bartimaeus obeyed the revelation of Jesus in his heart.

Bartimaeus' story applies to us too. Through a variety of mediums, we hear of Jesus, but rather than doing the things that we know we should do, we are content to sit in darkness while accepting handouts from others through the power of technology and media. And when we take it upon ourselves to do what we know to do (i.e., call out to Jesus), it is all too easy for those who should help us to instead try to silence us. However, like Bartimaeus, we cannot sit begging—we must trust and obey the level of knowledge that we have.

Depression, Where Is Your Sting?

I remember hearing about a young Christian woman back in Scotland who suffered from depression, but she did not seek help for it, not even medication. Her rationale was that she enjoyed being the person that the depression made her. She was artistic, into music, creative writing, and so forth, and she believed that depression added to her creativity. She thought that not having depression would turn her into someone whom she did not want to be.

I can associate with her line of thinking. When I suffered from my first bout of depression before I was saved, I was creative and wrote poetry and short stories. However, my creative inclination departed overnight when God saved me and healed me from depression. Although I was glad I never had depression anymore, I felt like a large part of me had gone. So, I can relate to this young woman. However, I was desperate—I would have paid any price to get rid of depression, even if that meant removing a part of me that I liked.

From my experience and from the experiences of depression sufferers with whom I talked, most would do anything to get rid of depression. Because of this, I sometimes wonder if the young woman suffered from depression at all. I am inclined to believe that rather than depression, she may have suffered from a lack of faith in God's ability to transform her into a more fulfilled person than she could imagine herself being. Although I heard of this woman many years ago now and do not know what became of her, I know that God has never left her life. Because God's inclination is to nurture his children, I believe this woman is now a more whole and fulfilled Christian than she was then.

As someone whom God has delivered and healed from depression twice, I believe that depression is not something with which any Christian has to live. I have found that instead of conforming to the image of the person that we want to be, the person into whom God would turn us is much greater than we could ever imagine. Although I felt that depression took away a part of me I liked, God gave more back to me and boosted me forward into a career where I get to think and write and do all the things that I thought depression helped me to do.

Sadly, many people become comfortable with the way things are. Then they share their stories with others who are in the same boat and thus create a false certainty about their situations. They conclude, "This is the way God sovereignly wants me to be." Their certainty, then, attracts other Christians who are dealing with similar things who think, "Maybe this is the way God sovereignly wants me to be too?"

Therefore, instead of hearing of the healing power of Jesus and the liberating truth of the Holy Spirit's work, these people create a stagnant group in which it is okay to be the way you are. Furthermore, Christians losing the same battle will flock to such people because of their own discouragement. Through time, then, they become happy being defined by the very thing they are supposed to be struggling against. They say, "Great, someone with whom I can identify: a Christian who is honest about their situation." They are, perhaps, honest about their struggles, but authentic hope is absent if they do not strive to let the Word of God define them and the Holy Spirit work in their lives.

There is some truth to the statement, "Deliverance is for the desperate." I have heard this saying many times throughout my Christin life. John Wimber and Kevin Springer say that desperation, or the lack thereof, is one of many reasons some do not receive healing. They write:

> There is another reason—I believe the most fundamental reason—why more people are not healed when prayed for today. We do not seek God as wholeheartedly as we should. In other words, God can do greater miracles than we have yet seen if only we would persist in seeking him.[2]

I always thought this quotation sounded like a get-out clause to explain why some people do not experience God's healing power. However, when I remember my salvation experience and how God healed me from depression and delivered me from vice, the fact is that I knelt for hours praying before I met God. Before kneeling, I resolved not to move until I knew for sure whether God existed. Because I sought God within that dilemma, he saved and healed me. I sometimes wonder what would have happened if I had prematurely given up. However, when I remember back to that point in my life, I was so desperate that there was no possibility of giving up. Even during my second bout of depression, when I recited the Psalms hour after hour in my spare room, I remembered the depths to which depression had taken me in the past. I determined that there was no way I was going back there. Because of this, I accidentally ended up obeying God's instruction to me and put into practice the solution to my problem.

---

2. Wimber and Springer, *Power Healing*, 158.

Depression, Where Is Your Sting?

OUR EXPERIENCES SANCTIFY US TO HELP OTHERS

In an earlier chapter, we spoke about how depression acted as a crucible experience for some people, causing positive changes in their lives. The idea was that if a person could positively process their experience of depression, then depression just might serve a purifying purpose that enriches their life and bears fruit. In that chapter, I pointed out that it is easy to look back on a horrible experience and see its value. Still, it is another thing to be stuck in the middle of that horrific experience and be able to process it as something that will ultimately be enriching. Overall, I disagreed somewhat with this theme, because I felt that formulating a positive outcome out of an experience typified by negative feelings, such as meaninglessness, apathy, suicide, abandonment, and deep darkness, was inconsistent with the experience itself. To me, the possibility of depression acting as a crucible that makes the sufferer a better person was an alien thought inconsistent with the pathology of the condition. However, now that I went through depression a second time as a Christian, I relate more favorably to depression as a crucible experience that can lead to fresh insights about God, one's life, and one's role in creation, all of which provide a richer experience of the Spirit. I now see how the crucible experience of depression fits in with a broader discussion of the role of Christian sanctification.

When I think of what I went through in the UK, I now see how it fits into the broader scheme of sanctification. Green describes how, by sharing in Christ's life and joining in his works, we learn obedience in the same way that Christ learned obedience (Matt 10:24; Heb 5:8–9).[3] Borrowing from John Wesley, Green says that although Jesus' atoning work was once and for all, and is more than enough for our salvation, Christians must likewise suffer and obey in imitation of their participation in the life of Christ. Green describes how, by God's grace, the Spirit takes our sufferings and cultivates them to bring to fruition the fullness of our sharing of the divine life.[4] Therefore, there is a redemptive aspect to our obedience and our suffering through which sanctification occurs, and we grow in Christlikeness. The fact that I would not trade my negative experiences at my local church in the UK nor my life experiences during this period for anything, shows that what I experienced during this period contributed to the Spirit's sanctifying work in my life. In many respects, I learned obedience. I thank God

---

3. Green, *Sanctifying Interpretation*, 15.
4. Green, *Sanctifying Interpretation*, 19–21.

that I never left to do my own thing and ran away from my local church. Instead, my wife and I waited for God's time, and he moved us on when he was ready to do so.

One day a visiting preacher who had a gift of prophecy came to our church as a guest speaker. He asked my wife and me to come up on stage, saying that the Lord had a word for us. To paraphrase, he said that those dreams we were trying to let die would not die, because they were from God. He explained that although the Lord had called us to lead and teach his people, he was waiting on our response. More precisely, God was waiting on my response, because as it happened, the preacher's prophecy corresponded to what my wife had been praying in private for months. Therefore, the call to respond was on me.

The preacher's confirmation of my life's purpose and my healing from depression using the Psalms at around that same time, coincided to bring this season of my life to a close. Shortly after this service, we moved out of the city to a larger home following our firstborn's arrival. Our church blessed us during our last service in attendance, and we moved to a small community thirty miles away, and we got plugged into a Pentecostal church there. We flourished in this new church, and my vision for ministry and God's call on my life came back. Accurate to the preacher's prophecy, I found a renewed purpose for my life, which culminated in receiving the church's blessing to follow the Lord to the USA to begin doctoral studies. The rest, as they say, is history.

According to Green, justification and sanctification find their fulfillment and fullness in a faithfully lived vocation.[5] He explains that because the Spirit unites our lives with Christ's life, we enter his vocation for the world and become holy witnesses empowered by the Spirit.[6] Through our cooperation with him, we bring the redemptive beauty of holiness to creation.[7] Green says that what Christ went through for us, we go through for Christ and each other.[8] These remarks reflect 2 Corinthians 1:3–6:

> Blessed be the God and Father of our Lord Jesus Christ, the Father of mercies and God of all comfort, who comforts us in all our tribulation, that we may be able to comfort those who are in any trouble, with the comfort with which we ourselves are comforted

---

5. Green, *Sanctifying Interpretation*, 22.
6. Green, *Sanctifying Interpretation*, 12–15.
7. Green, *Sanctifying Interpretation*, 32.
8. Green, *Sanctifying Interpretation*, 16.

by God. For as the sufferings of Christ abound in us, so our consolation also abounds through Christ. Now if we are afflicted, it is for your consolation and salvation, which is effective for enduring the same sufferings which we also suffer. Or if we are comforted, it is for your consolation and salvation.

I doubt I would have written this book had I not gone through these challenges in my life. Keener says that one hallmark of John the Evangelist's theology is that people do not understand God's purposes until they come to pass.[9] This is a correct observation of the Christian life in general. We often find it hard to discern the start from the finish during troublesome times, and we find it hard to understand precisely what is going on and why. But when we make it through to the other side, the Holy Spirit gracefully offers us a bird's-eye view. He brings all things to our remembrance (John 14:26), so we can look back and see how God's hand was on everything that we experienced and appreciate how we grew in Christlikeness during that period.

I began this book by showing pictures of my son's first time at the beach. When we went to the beach that day, we stood at the same place where I tried to commit suicide all those years before. I now have another two children, and my wife and I are enjoying living life in God's presence. My life is full of vitality and promise. The Spirit has blessed me with a bird's-eye view of that season of my life. Now when I look at those photos we took at the beach, my heart rejoices, and I triumphantly think, "O death, where is thy sting? O grave, where is thy victory?" (1 Cor 15:55 KJV). Or, in this case, "Depression, where is your sting?"

---

9. Keener, *The Gospel of John*, 530–31; 779.

Afterword

HEALING INVOLVES THE PROCESSES through which we reach a healthier state of wellbeing and encompasses both a natural and spiritual dynamic. In this book, I tried to narrate a little of my journey towards wholeness as it relates to depression while using some of my doctoral research as a supplement. My aim was never to write a self-help or a how-to book. Instead, I wanted to leave room for the Holy Spirit to speak so that the reader could follow the Spirit's guidance about their particular situation. However, I would have been amiss not to provide some pointers. Nothing that I wrote is prescriptive—but then, maybe it is a little prescriptive from a biblical standpoint. The fact is, what could be better than following King David's lead who, in a time before modern psychological and psychiatric treatments, found relief from his suffering in God. Even in depression, through the grace of the loving God who created us, sustains us, and brings us into an eternal relationship with him through Christ, we can find hope that transcends our circumstances. David knew this truth, and he clung to it throughout his life. Therefore, our first response in times of mental distress should be to seek God. God has given us the Psalms. Maybe we should use them. If David, a man after God's own heart, knew what to do when he suffered, then maybe we should follow suit.

Bibliography

Adams, Jay E. *The Christian Counselor's Manual*. Grand Rapids, MI: Ministry Resources Library, 1973.
American Psychiatric Association. *Diagnostic and Statistical Manual of Mental Disorders*. 5th ed. Washington, DC: American Psychiatric Association, 2013.
Altschule, Mark D. "The Two Kinds of Depression According to St. Paul." *The British Journal of Psychiatry* 113 (1967) 779–80.
Anderson, Alan A. *Introduction to Pentecostalism*. Cambridge, UK: CUP, 2014.
Asamoah-Gyadu, J. Kwabena. "Pulling down Strongholds: Evangelism, Principalities and Powers and the African Pentecostal Imagination." *International Review of Mission* 96 (2007) 306–17.
Ashbrook, B. J. "The Functional Meaning of the Soul in Christian Tradition." *Journal of Pastoral Theology* 13 (1958) 1–16.
Avenevoli, Shelli, et al. "Major Depression in the National Comorbidity Survey—Adolescent Supplement: Prevalence, Correlates, and Treatment." *Journal of the American Academy of Child and Adolescent Psychiatry* 54 (January 2015) 37–44.
Bardach, Naomi S., et al. "Common and Costly Hospitalizations for Pediatric Mental Health Disorders." *Pediatrics* 133 (April 2014).
Barnes, Elizabeth. *The Story of Discipleship*. Nashville, TN: Abingdon, 1995.
Beck, Aaron T., and Brad A. Alford. *Depression: Causes and Treatment*. Philadelphia: University of Pennsylvania Press, 2009.
Bergunder, Michael. "Miracle healing and exorcism: The South Indian Pentecostal movement in the context of popular Hinduism." *International Review of Mission* 90 (January 2001) 103–12.
Blazer, Dan G. *The Age of Melancholy: Major Depression and Its Social Origin*. Florence, UK: Routledge, 2005.
Bosch, David J. *Transforming Mission*. Maryknoll, NY: Orbis Books, 1996.
Boyd, Kenneth M. "Disease, Illness, Sickness, Health, Healing and Wholeness: Exploring Some Elusive Concepts." *Medical Humanities* 26 (June 2000) 9–17.
Brueggemann, Walter. *An Introduction to the Old Testament: The Canon and Christian Imagination*. Louisville: Presbyterian Publishing Corporation, 2003.
Brown, M. J. "Aquinas' Alternative to Cartesian Dualism (Updated)." *Truth is a Man: The Writings of J. Matthew Brown* (blog). https://jmatthanbrown.wordpress.com/2009/12/03/aquinas-alternative-to-cartesian-dualism/.
Burke, Trevor J. "Romans." In *A Biblical Theology of the Holy Spirit*, edited by Trevor J. Burke and Keith Warrington, 129–44. Eugene, OR: Cascade, 2014.

Bibliography

Chan, Simon. *Pentecostal Theology and the Christian Spiritual Tradition*. Eugene, OR: Wipf & Stock, 2011.

Child Trends Databank. "Adolescents Who Felt Sad or Hopeless." *Childtrends.org*, 2014. https://www.childtrends.org/wp-content/uploads/2016/03/indicator_1458653727.217.html.

Coudert, Allison P. "Melancholy, Madness, and Demonic Possession in the Early Modern West." In *Mental Health, Spirituality, and Religion in the Middle Ages and Early Modern Age*, edited by Albrecht Classen, 647–89. Boston: de Gruyter, 2014.

Cover, Robin. C. "Sin, Old Testament." In *Anchor Bible Dictionary* 6:31–40.

Davids, Peter H. *The Epistle of James: A Commentary of the Greek Texts*. New International Greek Testament Commentary. Grand Rapids, MI: Eerdmans, 1982.

Davis, Andrew M., et al. *Exalting Jesus in Isaiah: Christ-Centered Exposition*. Edited by David Platt et al. Tennessee: Holman Reference, 2017.

Dein, Simon, et al. "Theodicy and End-of-Life Care." *Journal of Social Work in End-of-Life and Palliative Care* 9 (2013) 191–208.

Depression and Bipolar Support Alliance. "Depression Statistics." *Dbsalliance.org*. https://secure2.convio.net/dabsa/site/SPageServer/?pagename=education_statistics_depression.

Dewing, Jan. "Personhood and Dementia: Revisiting Tom Kitwood's Ideas." *International Journal of Older People Nursing* 3 (February 2008) 3–13.

Dobson, James D. "Gifted for Change: The Evolving Vision for Tongues, Prophecy, and Other Charisms in American Pentecostal Churches." *Studies in World Christianity* 17.1 (2011) 50–71.

Durbin, Emily C. *Depression 101*. New York: Springer, 2013.

Engel, George L. "The Need for a New Medical Model: A Challenge for the Biomedical Model." *Holistic Medicine* 4 (1989) 37–53.

Fenton, Steve, and Azra Sadiq-Sangster. "Culture, Relativism and the Expression of Mental Distress: South Asian Women in Britain." *Sociology of Health and Illness* 18 (January 1996) 66–85.

Garfield, Ken. "A Church Invests in Mental Health in Response to Parishioners' Suffering." *Faithandleadership.com*. https://faithandleadership.com/church-invests-mental-health-response-parishioners-suffering.

Green, Chris E. W. *Sanctifying Interpretation: Vocation, Holiness, and Scripture*. Cleveland, TN: Center for Pentecostal Theology, 2015.

Guth, CJ. "An Insider's Look at the Gerasene Disciple (Mark 5:1–20): Biblical Interpretation from the Social Location of Mental Illness." *Journal of Religion, Disability & Health* 11 (December 2007) 61–70.

Hall, Beverly A. "The Psychiatric Model: A Critical Analysis of Its Undermining Effects on Nursing in Chronic Mental Illness." *Advances in Nursing Science* 18 (1996) 16–26.

Hart, Archibald D., and Catherine Hart Weber. *Unveiling Depression in Women*. Grand Rapids, MI: Fleming H. Revell, 2002.

Hauerwas, Stanley. *Suffering Presence: Theological Reflections on Medicine, the Mentally Handicapped, and the Church*. Notre Dame, IN: University of Notre Dame Press, 1986.

Helman, Cecil G. "Disease Versus Illness in General Practice." *The Journal of the Royal College of General Practitioners* 31 (September 1981) 548–52.

Bibliography

Iosif, Despina. "'I Saw Satan Fall like Lightning from Heaven': Illness as Demon Possession in the World of the First Christian Ascetics and Monks." *Mental Health, Religion & Culture* 14 (April 2011) 323–40. https://doi.org/10.1080/13674671003598832.

Jewett, Robert. *Romans: A Commentary*. Edited by Eldon Jay Epp. Minneapolis: Fortress, 2007.

Jones, Logan C. "The Psalms of Lament and the Transformation of Sorrow." *The Journal of Pastoral Care & Counseling* 61 (2007) 47–58.

Keener, Craig S. *The Gospel of John: 2 Volumes*. Grand Rapids, MI: Baker Academic, 2010.

———. *Spirit Hermeneutics*. Grand Rapids, MI: Eerdmans, 2016.

Klaus, Byron. "The Holy Spirit and Mission in Eschatological Perspective: A Pentecostal Viewpoint." *Pneuma* 27 (Fall 2005) 322–42.

Kleinman, Arthur, et al. "Culture, Illness, and Care: Clinical Lessons from Anthropologic and Cross-Cultural Research." *Focus: Journal of Lifelong Learning in Psychiatry* 4 (Winter 2006) 140–46.

Kruger, Paul A. "Depression in the Hebrew Bible: An Update." *Journal of Near Eastern Studies* 64 (2005) 187–92.

Leathard, Helen L. "Healing in the Christian Tradition." *Sacred Space* 4 (June 2009) 33–39.

Levack, Brian P. "The Horrors of Witchcraft and Demonic Possession." *Social Research* 81 (Winter 2014) 921–39.

Levison, John R. *Filled With the Spirit*. Grand Rapids, MI: Eerdmans, 2009.

LifeWay Research. "New Study of Acute Mental illness and Christian Faith." *Lifewayresearch.com*, 2020. https://lifewayresearch.com/mentalillnessstudy/.

———. "Study of Acute Mental Illness and Christian Faith: Research Report," *Lifewayresearch.com*, 2014. http://lifewayresearch.com/wp-content/uploads/2014/09/Acute-Mental-Illness-and-Christian-Faith-Research-Report-1.pdf.

Louw, D. J. "Space and Place in the Healing of Life: Towards a Theology of Affirmation in Pastoral Care and Counselling." *Verbum et Ecclesia* 29 (May 2008) 426–45.

Ma, Julie, and Wonsuk Ma. *Mission in the Spirit*. Oxford, UK: Regnum Books International, 2010.

Mansfield, Stephen. *Derek Prince: A Biography*. Lake Mary, FL: Charisma House, 2005.

McBain, Robert D. "Exploring the Silent Nature of Depression and Revealing Christianity's Interpretive Healing Qualities within the Local Church." DMin diss., Oral Roberts University, 2020.

McDougal, Joy Ann. "Sin." In *The Cambridge Dictionary of Christian Theology*, edited by Ian A. McFarland et al., 473–75. Cambridge, UK: Cambridge University Press, 2011.

McGrath, Ellen. "Child Abuse and Depression." *Psychologytoday.com*, June 9, 2016. http://www.psychologytoday.com/articles/200305/child-abuse-and-depression.

McKnight, Scot. *The Letter of James*. The New International Commentary on the New Testament. Grand Rapids, MI: Eerdmans, 2011.

Menzies, William. *Bible Doctrines: A Pentecostal Perspective*. Springfield, MI: Gospel Publishing House, 2015.

Moreland, J. P., and Scott B. Rae. *Body & Soul: Human Nature & the Crisis in Ethics*. Downers Grove: IVP Academic, 2000.

Morin, Amy. "Depression Statistics Everyone Should Know." *Verywellmind.com*. https://www.verywellmind.com/depression-statistics-everyone-should-know-4159056.

Mounce, William D. "Μαίνομαι." *Billmounce.com*. https://www.billmounce.com/greek-dictionary/mainomai.

BIBLIOGRAPHY

National Network of Depression Centers. "Get the Facts." *Nndc.org*, 2018. https://nndc.org/facts/.
Negele, Alexa, et al. "Childhood Trauma and Its Relation to Chronic Depression in Adulthood." *Depression Research and Treatment*. 2015.
Nelson, Pauline Brand. "My Father's Hands." In *Suffering*, edited by Robert B. Kruschwitz, 76–83. Christian Reflection: A Series in Faith and Ethics. Waco, TX: The Center for Christian Ethics, Baylor University, 2005.
Nelson, William B. *Daniel*. Understanding the Bible Commentary Series. Grand Rapids, MI: Baker, 2013.
Nemade, Rashmi, et al. "Historical Understandings of Depression." *Mentalhelp.net*. https://www.mentalhelp.net/articles/historical-understandings-of-depression/.
Niebuhr, Reinhold. *The Nature and Destiny of Man: A Christian Interpretation*. Vol. 1. London: Nisbet & Co., LTD, 1941.
Nydegger, Rudy. *Understanding and Treating Depression*. Titles in Abnormal Psychology. Westport, CT: Praeger, 2008.
Oberman, Hester E. "A Postmodern Perspective on Mental Health, Spirituality, and Religion." In *Mental Health, Spirituality, and Religion in the Middle Ages and Early Modern Age*, edited by Albrecht Classen, 690–711. Boston, MA: de Gruyter, 2014.
Peck, Alexander. "What Is Christian Spirituality?" *Spirituality-for-life.org*. spirituality-for-life.org/pdf-files/WhatIsChristianSpirituality.pdf.
Peters, Tom. *Science, Theology and Ethics*. Aldershot, UK: Ashgate, 2003.
Pilch, John J. "Disease." In *New Interpreter's Dictionary of the Bible*. Ministrymatters.com. https://www-ministrymatters-com.oralroberts.idm.oclc.org/library/#/nidb/eeb130749276e502d35a063757e27985/disease.html.
Rowe, Dorothy. *Depression: The Way Out of Your Prison*. New York: Brunner-Routledge, 2003.
Saddleback Church. "Hope for Mental Health." *Hope4mentalhealth.com*.
Schimelpfening, Nancy. "The History of Depression: Accounts, Treatments, and Beliefs through the Ages." *Verywellmind.com*, November 3, 2018. https://www.verywellmind.com/who-discovered-depression-1066770.
Schuman, Joel James, and Keith G. Meador. *Heal Thyself: Spirituality, Medicine, and the Distortion of Christianity*. New York: Oxford University Press, 2003.
Simpson, Amy. "Mental Illness: What Is the Church's Role?" *Qideas.org*. http://qideas.org/articles/mental-illness-what-is-the-churchs-role.
Sire, James. *The Universe Next Door*. Downers Grove, IL: InterVarsity, 1988.
Sklar, Jay. "Sin." In *The Oxford Encyclopedia of the Bible and Theology*. Oxford, UK: Oxford University Press, 2014.
Smietana, Bob. "Mental Illness Remains Taboo Topic for Many Pastors." *LifewayResearch.com*, September 22, 2014. https://lifewayresearch.com/2014/09/22/mental-illness-remains-taboo-topic-for-many-pastors/.
Spurgeon, Charles. "Psalm 42." Treasury of David, Christianity.com. https://www.christianity.com/bible/commentary.php?com=spur&b=19&c=42.
Stanford, Matthew S. *Grace for the Afflicted: A Clinical and Biblical Perspective on Mental Illness*. Downers Grove, IL: InterVarsity, 2017.
Stetzer, Ed. "The Church and Mental Health: What Do the Numbers Tell Us?" *The Exchange with Ed Stetzer* (blog), April 20, 2018. https://www.christianitytoday.com/edstetzer/2018/april/church-and-mental-health.html.

Stone, Roxanne, et al. "Pastor and Mental Health Advocate Jarrid Wilson Dies by Suicide." *Christianitytoday.com*, September 10, 2019. https://www.christianitytoday.com/news/2019/september/pastor-mental-health-advocate-jarrid-wilson-dies-suicide.html.
Sulmasy, Daniel P. "A Biopsychosocial-Spiritual Model for the Care of Patients at the End of Life." *The Gerontologist* 42.3 (2002) 24–33.
Swinton, John. "From Health to Shalom: Why the Religion and Health Debate Needs Jesus." In *Healing to All Their Flesh: Jewish and Christianity Perspectives on Spirituality, Theology, and Health*, edited by Keith G. Meador and Jeffrey S. Levin, 219–41. West Conshohocken, PA: Templeton, 2012.
———. "Healing Presence." In *Suffering*, edited by Robert B. Kruschwitz, 68–75. Christian Reflection: A Series in Faith and Ethics. Waco, TX: The Center for Christian Ethics, Baylor University, 2005.
———. *Spirituality and Mental Health Care: Rediscovering a "Forgotten" Dimension*. London: Jessica Kingsley, 2001.
———. "Understanding Health." Class PowerPoint from DR4060 Spirituality, Health, and Healing, University of Aberdeen, UK, Fall session 2011.
Swinton, John, and Harriet Mowat. *Practical Theology and Qualitative Research*. London: Student Christian Movement, 2011.
Taylor, Michael Alan, and Max Fink. *Melancholia: The Diagnosis, Pathophysiology and Treatment of Depressive Illness*. Cambridge, UK: Cambridge University Press, 2006.
Thiselton, Anthony. *A Shorter Guide to the Holy Spirit*. Grand Rapids, MI: Eerdmans, 2016.
Trice, Pamela D., and Jeffrey P. Bjorck. "Pentecostal Perspectives on Causes and Cures of Depression." *Professional Psychology: Research and Practice* 37 (June 2006) 283–94.
Vacek, Heather H. *Madness: American Protestant Responses to Mental Illness*. Waco, TX: Baylor University Press, 2015.
Vondey, Wolfgang. *Pentecostal Theology: Living the Fullness of the Gospel*. London: Bloomsbury, 2017.
Waltke, Bruce K., et al. *The Psalms As Christian Lament*. Grand Rapids, MI: Eerdmans, 2014.
Wells, Samuel, and George Sumner. *Esther and Daniel*. Brazos Theological Commentary on the Bible. Grand Rapids, MI: Brazos, 2013.
White, John. *The Masks of Melancholy: A Christian Physician Looks at Depression and Suicide*. Downers Grove, IL: InterVarsity, 1982.
Wilkinson, John. *The Bible and Healing: A Medical and Theological Commentary*. Grand Rapids, MI: Eerdmans, 1998.
Wimber, John, and Kevin Springer. *Power Healing*. New York: Harper & Row, 1987.
Yong, Amos. *Renewing Christian Theology*. Waco, TX: Baylor University Press, 2014.

www.ingramcontent.com/pod-product-compliance
Lightning Source LLC
Chambersburg PA
CBHW050825160426
43192CB00010B/1897